MYSTERIOUS DISAPPEARANCES

MYSTERIOUS DISAPPEARANCES

Daniel Cohen

Illustrated with photographs and old prints

DODD, MEAD & COMPANY
New York

PICTURE CREDITS

Illustrations in this book are used by permission and through the courtesy of the following: American Museum of Natural History, 100, 111; Atlantic Mutual Companies, 33; Library of Congress, 2, 105; The Peabody Museum of Salem, 36, 39; United Press International Photo, 4, 11, 14; U.S. Bureau of Ships, 56; U.S. Coast Guard Photo, 63, 65; U.S. Navy Photo, 54.

j 001, 94
C O H
c. 1

Library of Congress Cataloging in Publication Data

Cohen, Daniel.
      Mysterious disappearances.

      Includes index.
      SUMMARY: Discusses some famous or strange disappearances of people, ships, planes, lands, planet, civilizations, and other things and includes a chapter on mysterious appearances.
      1. Curiosities and wonders—Juvenile literature.
[1. Curiosities and wonders] I. Title.
AG243.C578   001.9′4   75–38352
ISBN 0–396–07298–4

For Jacko, who came back

Contents

MYSTERIOUS DISAPPEARANCES

1

Lost, Stolen, or Strayed

If you wanted to become famous you could do worse than to disappear, suddenly and mysteriously. The disappearance must be mysterious, for, in fact, thousands of people do "disappear" in one sense or another every year, and no one but their immediate families and the missing persons bureau ever seems to take much notice. But a mysterious disappearance, particularly of a moderately prominent person, is the sort of thing which captures the public imagination.

Take the case of Ambrose Bierce. Bierce, who lived from the mid-nineteenth to the early twentieth century, attained a modest degree of fame during his lifetime as a writer of bitter, ironic, short stories and aphorisms. His stories are occasionally reprinted even today, and some of them stand up quite well. But what most people seem to remember about Ambrose Bierce is that in 1913 he disappeared.

In a sense, Bierce's disappearance isn't all that mysterious. In 1913 he was seventy-one years old and in poor health. Yet he set off for Mexico, presumably to join up in some way in the Mexi-

Ambrose Bierce

can Revolution that was going on at the time. Bierce was no dedicated revolutionary; he just loved wars, and the Mexican Revolution was the closest war at hand. Clearly he knew that a man of his years and constitution was not likely to survive such an adventure. In fact, in a letter written shortly before his disappearance he said that he had wearied of his life and decided to go to Mexico to find "a soldier's grave or crawl off into some cave and die like a free beast."

Presumably, one way or another, this last wish was granted.

But we don't know exactly what happened to Ambrose Bierce. His body has never been found, and there is no authentic record of his last days. That mystery, minor though it may be, captured the public's imagination. One Bierce biographer complained: "The mystery surrounding the disappearance of Ambrose Bierce in 1913 has become encrusted with an outlandish accretion of fanciful stories, marvelous explanations and ingenious conjectures. The newspaper writing on the subject is already voluminous and shows no sign of abating."

Among the theories that have been put forth are that Bierce was shot on the orders of the Mexican leader, Pancho Villa, and that he wound up in Europe on the staff of Lord Kitchener, British commander during World War I. The second theory is demonstrably false; we cannot be so sure about the first. Speculation on the subject will undoubtedly continue.

During her lifetime Amelia Earhart was the world's foremost woman aviator (or aviatrix, as she was called in those days). Today she is most famous because, in 1937, she and her navigator, Frederick Noonan, disappeared in the South Pacific during an attempted round-the-world flight.

All throughout the earlier stages of the flight there had been

3

Frederick Noonan and Amelia Earhart

trouble with the twin-engine Lockheed 10. Earhart and Noonan were already exhausted by the ordeal of the journey, and they were on the most difficult leg of the flight, over a section of the Pacific Ocean dotted with only a few small islands. Planes do crash, even if they are handled by expert pilots, so the disappearance of Amelia Earhart and Frederick Noonan is not altogether surprising. But, as in the case of Bierce, no one knows exactly what happened, and that is what fascinates us.

Naturally, rumors and speculation abound. The most persistent rumor is that Amelia Earhart flew over islands occupied by the Japanese and was shot down. War had not yet broken out between the United States and Japan—that was still four years in the future. But the Japanese military was extremely active in the South Pacific islands, and hostility between the United States and Japan in the area was running high. Most of the rumors insist that Earhart and Noonan were actually captured by the Japanese and either died in a concentration camp or were executed as spies. Some theories hold that Amelia Earhart actually was a spy, and the round-the-world flight was just a cover story for checking out Japanese military bases in the Pacific from the air.

Not so very long ago a book was published which insisted that Amelia Earhart had never died at all, but was still alive and living in the United States under an assumed name. The woman whom the book identified as Amelia Earhart in disguise was furious at the identification. She insisted that she was not Amelia Earhart, and sued. She wasn't, and the disappearance of Amelia Earhart remains a mystery.

Dorothy Arnold's name would probably have been completely unknown beyond a fairly limited circle of wealthy New Yorkers if she had not gone for a walk down Fifth Avenue on the afternoon of December 12, 1910, and disappeared forever.

According to a contemporary newspaper account: "She disappeared from one of the busiest streets on earth, at the sunniest hour of a brilliant afternoon, with thousands within sight and reach, men and women who knew her on every side, and officers of the law thickly strewn in her path."

From the Arnold case one gets the distinct feeling that something is being covered up. Though the disappearance was investigated by the police, by private investigators, and by the newspapers, there appear to be large and puzzling gaps in the investigation. If Dorothy Arnold had come to what her family considered a "shameful end"—if, for example, she had sneaked off somewhere and killed herself—her family may well have had the wealth and power to hide that fact.

But we don't know. All we do know is that at two o'clock in

the afternoon Dorothy Arnold was chatting with her friend, Gladys King, outside Brentano's bookstore on Twenty-seventh Street and Fifth Avenue. After that, no one who knew or recognized Dorothy Arnold ever reported seeing her again. Every once in a while the New York police still get calls from people who say they have seen Dorothy Arnold—though if she is still alive she is over ninety.

People don't disappear just one by one either. Sometimes a whole bunch of them disappear all together—like the crew of the *Mary Celeste*. That most celebrated of all maritime disappearances will be discussed in detail in Chapter 3.

When a large number of mysterious disappearances seem to have taken place in a single area, the mystery is compounded. Just such an aura of mystery surrounds the Bermuda Triangle —far and away the most popular "true mystery" of the 1970s. But we're saving that one for Chapter 4.

In addition to people and planes and ships, other things are rumored to have disappeared under mysterious circumstances. Islands, continents, even a whole planet may be missing from our solar system. And there is a good deal of talk of lost civilizations, or of secrets known by the ancients that have been lost. All of this and more will be discussed in the chapters that follow. And finally we are going to try and see if there is any thread, any underlying theme, which ties it all together.

Why is it that disappearances fascinate us so? A variety of explanations have been offered. Here is mine. I think that disappearances fascinate us, at least in part, because most of us have had a brush with some sort of mystery.

Now I don't know anyone who has disappeared, nor have I disappeared myself, and don't intend to if I can help it. But plenty of things around me have disappeared. What seems to disappear most persistently is pencils—now I am not joking here—because pencils disappear at a rate that is not only alarming, it is downright spooky. A certain percentage of these missing pencils turn up behind bookcases or in other odd corners. Others are carried outside by children and dogs, are found on the front lawn or down the block. But that doesn't account for all the missing pencils—not by a long shot. And it doesn't account for the missing scissors, and combs, and spoons, and all the other common household objects that regularly disappear. What happens to all of these things?

I have occasionally fantasied that there is a small invisible creature in the house that steals all of these things and tucks them away in its lair. One day, my fantasy runs, I'm going to come upon this lair and be buried in an avalanche of pencils, scissors, combs, spoons, and all the rest.

Have you ever had something disappear mysteriously, and then turn up again just as mysteriously? This has happened to me dozens of times, but one incident stands out in my mind.

I was looking for a book that I owned called *The Hittites* by O. R. Gurney. The Hittites were an ancient civilization of Asia Minor, and I needed information on them for something that I was writing. My books are arranged roughly by categories, so I went to the place where the book on the Hittites should have been, the place where I remembered seeing it just a few days before. It wasn't there.

That wasn't too surprising. I assumed it had been misplaced, so I looked through all the other shelves of history books, and still couldn't find it. So I looked through all the bookshelves—nothing. Then I began to search other places in the house where books are commonly left, then places where books were

7

never left, on the outside chance it might be there, all without success. It was a highly frustrating quest and consumed the better part of a day.

Had someone borrowed the book and failed to return it? That seemed impossible because I never lend out books. Besides, I don't know anyone, aside from myself, who has the slightest interest in the Hittites.

Finding the book became something of an obsession. For weeks I might take out an hour or so during the day to look for it, generally reexamining places that I had searched before.

Finally, though, I had to admit defeat—the book had disappeared and I had no idea how. So I went out and purchased another copy. I placed it on the shelf in the appropriate history section, and suddenly noticed that there were now two copies on the shelf, side by side. The book that I had searched for so long and so fruitlessly was back on the shelf, just where it should have been, just where I first looked for it, and right next to where I automatically placed its duplicate. For one eerie moment, I felt as if I had had a brush with the supernatural.

Was my missing book like the purloined letter in the Edgar Allan Poe story—something that was so obvious that it was simply overlooked? Could I possibly have stared at that exact spot, not once but a hundred times over several weeks, and not seen the book? Though I hate to admit it, it's possible that I am that unobservant. Still, every once in a while I get the feeling that the book disappeared for an unknown reason and then reappeared again for an equally unknown reason.

Most of you, I'm sure, have had similar experiences. But now it's time to turn from the homey world of disappearing pencils and books to grander mysteries.

2

They Never Came Back

The case of the mysterious disappearance of Judge Crater is not as well known as it used to be.

At one time the name evoked instant recognition throughout America. For years people investigated the case, speculated on it, and argued over it. So much work and so many words were poured into the search for Judge Crater—with so little success —that finally the case became something of a joke. During the 1930s and 1940s Judge Crater gags became standard in comedy routines.

As late as the 1960s Judge Crater jokes were still around. I can recall seeing two Judge Crater cartoons published in the early sixties. The first showed an astronaut stepping out of a space capsule on the moon and being greeted by a man in an old-fashioned business suit. The caption read "Hello there, I'm Judge Crater." The second cartoon showed a startled scientist looking through a microscope and saying to a colleague, "I think I've just discovered Judge Crater."

For over twenty years the disappearance of Justice Joseph

Force Crater of the Supreme Court of the State of New York was the most famous disappearance in America, perhaps in all the world. Though time may have dimmed public memory of the event, the case has never been solved. The total disappearance of Judge (really Justice, but that title never stuck) Crater remains a very good and very mysterious disappearance.

Judge Crater's final known appearance on this earth took place in New York City on the evening of August 6, 1930. Crater had dinner with some friends at the Billy Haas Restaurant at 332 West Forty-fifth Street. It was in the heart of the theater district, and the Justice announced his intention of going over to the Belasco Theater to see the hit show *Dancing Partner*. He had a ticket waiting for him at the box office. He was seen to leave the restaurant, hail a cab and get in, though the theater was only a block away. Someone picked up the ticket that had been left in Crater's name, but the man at the box office could not recall whether it was Crater or not, so we do not know if Judge Crater ever saw *Dancing Partner*. We do know that no one ever saw Judge Crater again—certainly not anyone who was willing to talk about it.

What made the disappearance so sensational was that Judge Crater really was an important man. He had been born in Easton, Pennsylvania, but studied law at Columbia University in New York City, and set up practice in the city. He rose rapidly, partly through his legal skill, but more significantly through his political skill. He was fascinated by the rough-and-tumble world of New York City politics, and he was able to play the game as well as anyone. While he taught law at Fordham University and served as law clerk to Supreme Court Justice and later Senator Robert Wagner, Crater's real power came from being president of the Cayuga Democratic Club, an

10

Justice Joseph Force Crater

Upper West Side Manhattan bulwark of Tammany Hall, the political power center of the city.

For years Tammany Hall had been flying high. Times had been good and if the politicians stole a bit here and there no one seemed to care very much. But in October, 1929, the stock

11

market collapsed and the Great Depression gathered steam. As prosperity disappeared so did some of the tolerance for crooked politics. Investigations began and several Tammany stalwarts found themselves out of office and in jail.

Early in 1930 a justice of the Supreme Court retired, and it was up to Governor Franklin D. Roosevelt to appoint a temporary successor. It was a ticklish problem in scandal-racked New York City and Roosevelt turned to Senator Wagner for advice. Wagner recommended his law secretary, Joseph Force Crater, for the job. Though Crater was a loyal Tammany man the appointment was generally applauded, for Wagner was well respected and no scandal had touched Crater—yet.

In November, 1930, Crater would have to stand for election to a full fourteen-year term on the State Supreme Court bench, and he was fully prepared to do so. It was said that he had his eye on ultimate appointment to the United States Supreme Court. He was only forty-one, young to be on the State Supreme Court, and his dream of going to the highest court in the land was not an impossible one—that is, if he had not disappeared.

Summer in New York City can be unbearably hot. It threatened to be even hotter for the newly created Justice in 1930, for the press uncovered the fact that Crater had been the principal speaker at a dinner for a man who was suspected of buying appointment to the post of magistrate in New York City's Traffic Court. It wasn't a major scandal, but it was a distinct embarrassment, coming on the heels of his own appointment. So Judge Crater and his wife Stella moved up to their summer cottage in Belgrade Lakes near Augusta, Maine. From time to time during the summer he made trips to New York City.

Crater returned from one of these trips on August 1, and was expected to remain at the cottage until the end of the month

12

when the fall term of the court was to begin. But the day after he got back he received a phone call—from whom we do not know. He mumbled something to his wife like, "I've got to straighten those fellows out," and then told her that he would have to go back to New York again the next day, but that he would return to Maine on August 9.

He arrived back in the city by train on the fourth and went to his apartment on Fifth Avenue, one of two he rented in the city. There Crater found the sleep-in maid and suggested to her that she take a four-day vacation until August 8, the day he planned to leave for Maine. Later that day he visited his doctor. The reason for his visit has never been made public.

He spent most of the following day in his judicial chambers apparently doing routine work.

The following day—the fatal sixth of August—Judge Crater again went to his chambers. He did behave in a rather unusual manner at that time. He asked one of his two assistants to cash a couple of checks for him. The checks totaled $5,100, a far more substantial sum in those days than today. He told the assistant to get large bills, and when given the money in an envelope, he slipped the envelope into his pocket without bothering to count the cash. He had also removed a large number of papers from his personal files. There were so many papers that they overflowed his briefcase. He borrowed an assistant's briefcase, but that still wasn't enough, and some of the papers had to be tied together in a large bundle.

Crater then asked his assistant, Joseph L. Mara, to help him get the papers to his Fifth Avenue apartment. The two men carried the papers to a cab. Later Mara told investigators that the usually cheerful Crater seemed "very blue and moody, evidently depressed and worried about something." But during

13

the cab ride he told Mara that he was going to Westchester for a swim that afternoon, and that he would see him tomorrow.

Whether Crater actually went for a swim that afternoon we do not know. There is no trace of his movements from noon to 7:00 P.M. Nor is there any indication of what happened to the large bundle of papers the Justice had removed from his chambers.

Crater's trail can be picked up again when at approximately 7:00 P.M. he appeared at the Arrow Theater Ticket Agency trying to get a single seat for that night's performance of *Dancing Partner*. He was told that tickets were hard to come by, and the agency had none on hand. However, the ticket agent assured him that if he were to go to the box office shortly before

Judge Crater and his wife at their summer home in Maine three days before he returned to New York and disappeared.

curtain time he would find a ticket waiting in his name.

Crater then strolled over to the popular Billy Haas Restaurant where he encountered a friend, William Klein, a lawyer who worked for major broadway producers. With Klein was a showgirl named Sally-Lou Ritz. Klein asked the Justice to join them for dinner. According to Klein, the dinner was unremarkable. Crater seemed in a good mood, and mentioned that he would be going back to Maine in a day or two.

After dinner Crater announced that he was going to see *Dancing Partner*. And here is one of the many oddities in the case. Crater left the restaurant at nine-fifteen, the curtain on *Dancing Partner* had already gone up, yet he had been told to arrive before curtain time to pick up his ticket.

If Crater himself had picked up the ticket, then he would have done so nearly an hour *after* curtain time. Yet the man in the box office professed not to remember who had picked up the ticket. Nor could the cab driver who had taken the Justice around the block to the Belasco Theater, or to somewhere else, ever be located, despite numerous appeals by the police and the New York newspapers.

What makes the matter of Judge Crater's disappearance even stranger is that the man was, to put the matter bluntly, funny looking. He was six-feet tall, a well-above-average height in 1930. He was fairly heavyset, but possessed an absurdly small head and neck, of which he was acutely self-conscious. He affected high, starched collars, but they didn't really hide the oddity. One writer described Crater as looking "something like a turtle walking upright." In addition, he had false teeth, and was wearing a bandage on his hand, for he had smashed a finger in a car door earlier in the summer. He was also quite a well-known figure around New York City, certainly not the sort who could easily melt into a crowd. Yet he disappeared, though it was a while before anyone seemed to realize this.

Up in Maine, Mrs. Stella Crater began to worry when her husband failed to return as scheduled on August 9. He had not telephoned or telegraphed that he would be late, though he was normally very considerate in such matters. Yet she waited six days before doing anything, and the first thing she did was send the family chauffeur to New York to see what he could find out. The chauffeur went to the Fifth Avenue apartment and talked to the maid. She said that after returning to work on the eighth she had found the Justice's bed rumpled, but could not determine when he had last slept there—had it been on the night of the sixth? The chauffeur began telephoning Crater's close friends, and though none of them knew where the Justice was they were full of reassurances that everything was all right. The chauffeur went back to Maine, and for a while nothing happened, though rumors of Crater's disappearance began to circulate.

The rumors became worse when Crater failed to show up at the opening of court on August 26. His political cronies began an informal investigation. They were extremely anxious to keep stories of mysterious disappearances out of the newspapers, for there was to be an election in less than three months. But when no information could be turned up by September 3—nearly a month after the disappearance of Judge Crater—they were finally forced to go officially to the police. The police already unofficially knew about the disappearance but had done nothing. Of course, the newspapers had a field day with the story.

Among his Tammany colleagues Judge Crater was known as "good old Joe Crater," a hearty backslapper who loved a good time. Just what sort of good time was revealed in the police investigation. They found that Crater had a long series of brief affairs with showgirls, and one long-term extramarital relationship with a woman named Constance Braemer Marcus. Connie Marcus had been a worker for Crater's Cayuga Democratic Club, and he had been the lawyer in her divorce. Over the years Crater visited Connie Marcus several times a week. He contributed a regular $60 to $70 toward her monthly rent of an apartment. Connie Marcus talked freely about Crater, but was no help at all in locating him.

Crater was also found to have been a regular customer at a Broadway speakeasy called the Club Abbey. Among the club's other regular customers were such prohibition-era gangsters as Dutch Schultz, and "Legs" Diamond. At the Abbey, Crater apparently called himself Joe Crane, but since so many other politicians frequented the place this bit of deception could hardly have been very successful.

An investigation of Crater's financial affairs was less sensational. He had several bank accounts, and a safe-deposit box. But no large sums of money were found, and there was no evidence that his accounts had ever contained large sums of money. All in all, he seemed to have no assets other than those that he could have acquired more or less legally as a lawyer and judge.

That was all that the investigation ever revealed. Later Mrs. Crater was to charge that the police had bungled the investigation, perhaps deliberately because of political interference. And that is certainly possible—more than possible. Yet Mrs. Crater herself was less than forthcoming, or else she knew incredibly little about her husband's life and work.

But even if the police had been working as hard as they could, their investigation would have been greatly hampered by the fact that there was a delay of nearly four weeks before the Justice's disappearance was officially reported. Whatever trail there may have been would have grown cold by that time.

In the absence of hard facts there are plenty of theories. The most obvious one is that Judge Crater disappeared because he wanted to. Law enforcement officials have often stated that most mysterious disappearances are really voluntary.

Some of Crater's actions before he disappeared certainly make it look as though he were planning something drastic. Taking money out of his bank, purging his personal papers, his odd carelessness about arriving at the theater are all highly suggestive. But why would he have wanted to disappear? The various scandals about his love life and associations would not have come to light at all if he had not disappeared in the first place. The bodies investigating corruption in New York City politics had nothing significant on Crater. His record was certainly not clean, but he seemed in no imminent danger of disgrace either.

One theory that was put forth by the sensationalist newspaper, the *New York Mirror*, was that Crater, disgusted with the life he was leading, had undergone some sort of religious conversion. He was born a Methodist but, said the *Mirror*, he had converted to Catholicism and ran off to an isolated monastery in Mexico. An intriguing notion, but one for which there is no supporting evidence whatever.

The other major theory is that Judge Crater's disappearance was involuntary—that he was kidnapped and murdered and his body effectively disposed of. Some of the fellows Crater met at the Club Abbey were perfectly capable of murder and well-practiced in dumping bodies in the East River, or hauling them upstate to one of the many unofficial burying grounds used by gangsters. But again the question arises, why? Professional gangsters do not kill without a reason, and they certainly would not have lightly killed a Justice of the State Supreme Court. Murders like that inevitably attract unwelcome publicity.

Another possibility is that his death was more or less accidental. One suggestion was that he died of a heart attack while in a house of prostitution. Those who ran the house—so this theory goes—panicked and disposed of the body. But why not just dump it on the street, since his death had been from natural causes?

Perhaps he was killed in a holdup—but what happened to the body? It is highly unlikely that a holdup man would drag a heavy corpse (Crater weighed 190 pounds) all over town looking for a good place to get rid of it. The disposal of Crater's body, if indeed there was a body to be disposed of, must have taken careful planning and a degree of expertise.

The theory that seems to make the most sense is that Crater went to meet some crooked associates on an important matter, perhaps blackmail. That fits with destroying papers, getting money, and apparently preparing some sort of alibi with the theater. During the meeting there was an argument in which Crater was killed. In haste the body was disposed of, and the murderers were lucky that it was never found. But who were these associates? What were they meeting about?

The mysterious disappearance of Judge Crater is one of those cases in which one feels that evidence may still possibly be revealed, even though it took place nearly half a century ago. If, as appears entirely likely, there was some sort of cover-up involved in the case, then memoirs, diaries, letters, or perhaps even official files, which could be made public only after all the participants in the affair were long dead and thus beyond pun-

19

ishment or censure, might provide new insights to the disappearance.

It seems unlikely that there will be any new evidence forthcoming in the case of Benjamin Bathurst, though the disappearance of Bathurst had the sort of notoriety in the nineteenth century that the Judge Crater case attained in the twentieth.

Bathurst was last seen in November, 1809, in a small German town where he was stopping on his way back to England. His coach for the journey was being prepared, and he was checking the horses. Two people reported seeing him walk around to the far side of the coach, but no one ever reported seeing him again.

Like Judge Crater, Bathurst was a prominent fellow, certainly not the sort who might disappear without creating quite a stir. Bathurst came from a well-to-do family, and though only in his twenties, he had been entrusted with a number of important diplomatic missions. One of them—his last as it turned out—was an attempt to persuade Austria to invade France as part of a campaign against Napoleon. Bathurst's mission was successful, though how significant his particular efforts were is a matter of speculation. The Austrians crossed the French border, were thoroughly defeated, and forced to capitulate in October of 1809.

Bathurst had remained in Vienna throughout the entire disasterous affair, but after a peace between Austria and France had been concluded he made plans to return to England. The shortest way home lay directly through France, but Bathurst was apprehensive. Though England and France were not at the time technically at war, Bathurst felt that Napoleon might hold a grudge over the part he had played in getting the Austrians to go to war, and would somehow harm him if he entered French territory.

Henry, Earl Bathurst, father of the missing Benjamin Bathurst.

Whether he had any real grounds for this fear is unknown, but he contrived to go home the long way, through the German territories. He even made an attempt to disguise his identity, calling himself Mr. Koch, a German commercial traveler. He also constantly kept two loaded pistols in his possession.

At about noon on November 25, 1809, Benjamin Bathurst reached the little German town of Perleberg. He announced his intention to rest and dine in the town before continuing his journey at about 7:00 P.M. Testimony concerning Bathurst's movements after his arrival in Perleberg is confusing and often contradictory, but the main outlines can be sketched.

21

He seems to have gone to the house of a Captain Klitzing, who was the military governor of Perleberg. There, without revealing his identity, he said that he was afraid that French spies were plotting against his life, and he asked for military protection. He seemed very upset. Klitzing thought that the young man was the victim of an overactive imagination, but he still agreed to send two soldiers to the post house where Bathurst's carriage was being readied.

On leaving Captain Klitzing, Bathurst apparently went back to the post house and ordered his carriage for nine o'clock in the evening instead of seven, which was the hour he had previously arranged to set out. He then went to an inn called the White Swan where he had taken a room, and spent several hours looking over his correspondence, burning certain letters and writing others. He finished at 7:00 P.M. when it was quite dark.

Then he did something quite foolish and inexplicable for a man who claimed to be in mortal fear for his life. He dismissed the two soldiers and sent them back to Captain Klitzing. Shortly before nine o'clock he went to the post house, where he spent a bit of time standing in front of the fire. A few minutes before his intended departure he left the post house to check his horses and carriage. The last persons to report seeing him were two employees of the post house who were holding the horses.

Just how long it was before those at the post house became seriously concerned by Bathurst's disappearance is not clear. It couldn't have been very long, for the horses and carriage were ready to go. At first it was assumed that he had gone back to the inn, but when his room was found to be empty, Captain Klitzing was informed. A wide search was then organized, but Benjamin Bathurst was never found.

Though Bathurst had openly expressed fear of French agents, it was initially suspected that his disappearance had come about through more conventional means—that he was robbed and murdered by someone who knew or cared nothing of his true identity. He was richly dressed when he arrived in Perleberg, and there were plenty around who might have murdered him for the clothes on his back.

Captain Klitzing immediately favored this theory, and he found support for it. Augustus Schmitz, ne'er-do-well son of the owner of the post house, was found in possession of Bathurst's overcoat. Schmitz freely admitted stealing the coat, but said he had no idea whose coat he had stolen. Bathurst had not been wearing the coat at the time he disappeared; it was stolen after he disappeared. There were other rumors that some of Bathurst's possessions had been seen on the person of this or that disreputable character in the vicinity of Perleberg. None of these accusations was ever proven, and most of them were probably the result of malicious gossip.

Inevitably the idea that Bathurst had been kidnapped by the French attracted far more attention. On December 16 a peasant woman found a pair of trousers, turned inside out, on a little path near Perleberg. The trousers were identified as those that Benjamin Bathurst wore at the time of his disappearance. On their being examined, two bullet holes were found, but no traces of blood. In one of the pockets was a half-written letter in Bathurst's handwriting. It was addressed to his wife in England and expressed fears concerning a certain Count D'Entraigues, and doubts as to whether he would ever get back to England. In case of his death he implored his wife not to marry again.

This discovery merely complicated the problem. If Bathurst had been shot by French spies, why had no one heard the shots on the night he had disappeared? And more importantly, why had his body been dragged off, while his pants containing the incriminating letter had been left behind? We must also remember that Bathurst was young, strong, well-armed, and on his guard. It would not have been easy to take him without a noisy struggle.

Bathurst's wife was convinced that somehow or other Napoleon was responsible for her husband's disappearance. She heard a rumor that an unknown Englishman was imprisoned in Magdeburg Fortress. She rushed to Magdeburg where she met the governor of the Fortress. He readily admitted that he once had an Englishman as prisoner. But he said that the man was named Louis Fritz and that he was a spy in the employ of George Canning, a member of the British government. When she asked to see this Louis Fritz, the governor said that was impossible since he had been released and gone to Spain. Canning later denied ever having employed a spy named Louis Fritz.

Mrs. Bathurst was then contacted by Count D'Entraigues, the man that her husband had alluded to so ominously in his final letter. The count's story was that Bathurst had not only been imprisoned in Magdeburg, but had been executed there on the orders of Joseph Fouchet, minister of police in Paris and master of intrigue and spying. The execution the count implied had been something of an accident, for they had not realized the importance of the man seized, thinking him an ordinary British spy. In order to cover up the error Fouchet, along with the governor of Magdeburg, invented the story of Louis Fritz. The count offered to supply positive evidence of the execution of Bathurst, but before he could do so he and his wife were stabbed to death by a French footman, who had apparently gone berserk.

Was the murderous footman another of Fouchet's agents? Indeed, who was Count D'Entraigues in the first place? It seems he too was a spy, but for which side—the French or English? The best guess is that he was a spy for both sides—so it is quite impossible to surmise his motives.

The French struck back at the accusations that they had done away with Bathurst. Several French newspapers stated that Bathurst had killed himself, probably in a fit of insanity. "It is the custom of the British Cabinet," remarked the *Moniteur* of January 29, 1810, "to commit diplomatic commissions to persons whom the whole nation knows are half fools."

The *Moniteur* failed to speculate as to how Benjamin Bathurst, after killing himself, managed to hide his own body.

Another suggestion was that Bathurst, in mortal fear for his life, arranged his own disappearance but was later killed some distance from Perleberg perhaps by robbers. Another possibility was that Bathurst in disguise got to the coast and was drowned when the ship in which he was crossing to England sank. In those days a sea crossing from the Continent to England was till a pretty chancy business, particularly in late November.

The charge that Bathurst suddenly went mad sounds an absurd one at first. And yet, there seems something quite overwrought about his fear of being killed by the French. The war with Austria was over and settled very much on French terms. Bathurst could not or should not have been carrying any documents that would have been of any interest to Napoleon any more. What, then, was he burning before he disappeared? Was his fear of the French a paranoid reaction? Or was he in reality afraid of someone else—but who, and why?

The disappearance of Benjamin Bathurst continued to be the subject of public discussion for many years. The Bathurst family offered rewards for information, and traced every promising lead. They came up with nothing.

In 1852, forty-two years after Benjamin Bathurst's disappearance, a human skeleton was found under the floor of a house in Perleberg that was being demolished. That news sent Bathurst's sister to Germany. A local physician examined the skeleton, and checked it against a portrait of Bathurst. He said there was no possibility that the skeleton had belonged to the missing man, and the sister agreed.

The case of Benjamin Bathurst is full of oddities and contradictions. All that we really know for sure is that after the evening of November 25, 1809, he was seen no more.

The mysterious disappearances of Benjamin Bathurst and Judge Crater have become classic cases because the individuals involved were prominent, and because a fair amount is known about the circumstances surrounding each case. But as we have already noted, thousands upon thousands of people "disappear" every year. Some of these disappearances may be genuinely mysterious, but it is difficult to tell, for the scanty details of the case may appear only in a hastily written police record or a brief newspaper story. There may be little or no follow-up.

What, for example, is one to do with this story, picked at random from a huge number that I have examined. It comes from the *Chicago Tribune* of January 5, 1900:

"Sherman Church, a young man employed in the Augusta Mills (Battle Creek, Mich.) has disappeared. He was seated in the company's office when he rose and ran into the mill. He has not been seen since. The mill has been almost taken to pieces by the searchers, and the river, woods, and country have been scoured, but to no avail. Nobody saw Church leave town, nor is there any known reason for his doing so."

Did Sherman Church disappear of his own free will, or was he carried off? Did he disappear at all or was the whole story an exaggeration, a mistake, or a deliberate hoax? There are no answers to any of these questions. Yet after reading a large number of such stories, one begins to get the slightly uncomfortable feeling that it is possible to step out on the street, or walk around the corner, and disappear. That is, of course, a totally unjustified feeling—for the really good cases of mysterious disappearances are quite rare. Mercifully so, for who wants to disappear? Those incidents in which all the information seems to come from a single unsubstantiated clipping or two should really be ignored as unworthy of the attention of the serious connoisseur of real mysteries. Yet there is one that I really can't help passing on, because it too has become a classic of sorts.

The account appeared in the London Sunday *Express* of September 21, 1924. It concerned the disappearance of two British airmen that had taken place in the Middle East some months earlier.

The Middle East was undergoing one of its apparently endless series of political and military crises. At the time, the British exercised considerable influence in the area. Flight Lieutenant W. T. Day and Pilot Officer D. R. Stewart were sent from British headquarters on an ordinary reconnaissance over the desert. The men did not return as scheduled and they were searched for. The plane was located with relative ease in the desert. But why had it set down in the first place? "There was some petrol left in the tank. There was nothing wrong with the craft. It was, in fact, flown back to the aerodrome," the *Express* reported. There had been no unusual meteorological conditions that might have forced the plane to land. Nor was there any indication that the plane had been shot at. Yet it had landed and the men were gone.

Stranger, still, is that in the sand around the plane searchers found the footprints of Day and Stewart. "They were traced, side by side, for some forty yards from the machine. Then, as suddenly as if they had come to the brink of a cliff, the marks ended."

So, unfortunately, does the information on this particular story.

3

Ghost Ships

No book of mysterious disappearances could possibly be complete without the tale of the *Mary Celeste*. It is the classic tale of a disappearance at sea, and what is more, unlike some other popular mysteries, it really is mysterious.

The basics of the story can be told simply enough. Early in the afternoon of December 5, 1872, the British brigantine *Dei Gratia*, sailing approximately halfway between the Azores and the coast of Portugal, sighted another brigantine. The ship was clearly in trouble, moving erratically with part of her sails blown away.

Dei Gratia captain David Reed Morehouse looked through his telescope but could see no one on deck, so he decided to send out a boarding party. It was no easy task. The *Dei Gratia* was a difficult ship to handle and the weather was heavy, but finally the British brigantine got close enough to the drifter to be able to send out a small boat with a party of three. The drifter turned out to be the American ship, *Mary Celeste*. The boarding party found, to their amazement, that the ship was absolutely empty.

The yawl, a small boat carried by the *Mary Celeste*, was gone. So were the chronometer and sextant, two important navigational instruments, and the ship's papers, including the register. The logbook, however, was still in the captain's cabin. The last entry, dated November 24, gave no hint of trouble. It stated simply, "about 110 miles due west of the island of Santa Maria in the Azores."

In some accounts of the *Mary Celeste* mystery it has been said that plates with food on them were found in the galley. This is not so; all plates and food were properly stowed, as they would have been between meals. But there was plenty of other evidence that the ship had been abandoned in great haste. Most impressive to the searchers from the *Dei Gratia* was that they found the captain's books and greatcoat, and all the sailors' personal possessions, including their pipes and tobacco, still on board. These were things that no seaman would leave behind unless in immediate and mortal fear for his life.

So the ship was abandoned some time after November 24— that seemed clear enough. What was not so clear, and what constitutes the mystery of the *Mary Celeste*, is why she was abandoned at all. Abandoning a ship in mid-ocean was not a common occurrence, but it was not unknown either, and the *Mary Celeste* was not the only ship that had been found empty and drifting in the sea. The most common reason for abandonment was that the ship had been damaged because of a storm or a fire on board, and was feared to be in danger of sinking.

But such was not the case with the *Mary Celeste*. The ship had been battered by the waves in the days she had drifted, abandoned. But she was completely seaworthy. This was proved beyond a doubt by three men from the *Dei Gratia* who took over the ship, and in two days put her in shape to sail to Gibraltar, easily weathering a severe storm along the way.

Another, though less common reason for abandoning a ship, was piracy or mutiny. Pirates would kill or capture the crew, leaving the ship to drift. Mutineers might wish to escape the scene of the crime. But neither seemed likely in the least. In either case there would certainly have been a struggle, and some signs of it would be found on the ship. There were none. Either pirates or mutineers would have taken more than the navigational instruments and the ship's registry. Certainly mutinous sailors would not have left behind their pipes. There seemed no possible reason why anyone should have left the *Mary Celeste*, yet everyone was gone.

Clearly the story is a strange one, but in order to fully appreciate its strangeness we must back up a bit, to the time that the *Mary Celeste* was built. She had been built in Nova Scotia in 1861, and christened *Amazon*. From the beginning she was a hard-luck ship. Her first master died just a few days after the ship was christened. On her first trip down the Maine coast she struck a fishing weir and was damaged. During her maiden voyage to Europe she ran into a brig in the Straits of Dover, sinking the other ship.

In 1867 it looked as though *Amazon* had come to a quick and inglorious end. She ran aground on Cape Breton Island, and was considered a total wreck. But the remains were sold to a man named McBean who reconditioned her, renamed her *Mary Celeste*, and then went broke.

The *Mary Celeste* wound up in the hands of James H. Winchester, owner of a New York shipping firm. He once again refurbished the ship, and brought her to tip-top shape and turned her over to Captain Benjamin Spooner Briggs of Marion, Massachusetts. He was to serve as master of the vessel, and also

31

owned a small interest in it—a fairly common practice for ships' captains in those days.

At the time he took over the *Celeste*, Captain Briggs was thirty-eight years old, but he had spent most of those years at sea. He came from a seafaring family, and became a master mariner when quite young. He had already captained three other ships, and had the reputation of being a solid, sober, industrious captain.

In November of 1872 the *Celeste* was tied up at a pier on New York's East River. She was being loaded with a cargo of casks of commercial alcohol, for shipment to Genoa, Italy.

At a nearby pier was the British brigantine *Dei Gratia*, taking on a mixed cargo and bound for Gibraltar. Briggs and the *Dei Gratia* master, David Reed Morehouse, were old friends. They dined together at the Astor House on the night of November 3. If Briggs had any anxiety about his ship or eight-member crew he did not express it at the time. On the contrary, he seemed well pleased with both, and planned to take his wife and infant daughter along on the voyage. Despite much that has been written about sailors' superstitions concerning having women on a voyage, it was quite common for captains to take their wives and children.

The *Mary Celeste* embarked from New York on November 5. Severe headwinds forced her to anchor off Staten Island for two days, then she set off into the North Atlantic. The *Dei Gratia* embarked on November 11. Twenty-four days later the two ships met in mid-ocean in what has grown to be one of the most publicized encounters in naval history.

Whatever Captain Morehouse may have felt about the disappearance of his old friend Captain Briggs, he was not too distressed to think of his own profit. He had located an abandoned

The Dei Gratia *sights the abandoned* Mary Celeste.

ship in mid-ocean, and under the salvage laws he could claim part of the value of the ship and its cargo. This meeting with the *Celeste* promised to result in a handsome profit.

All this looked suspicious to the authorities in Gibraltar, and within two hours of the time the *Celeste* was brought into port the authorities attached her and her cargo, until a hearing could be held before the Vice-Admiralty court. At stake was not only a valuable ship and cargo, but quite possibly the life and liberty of the captain and crew of the *Dei Gratia*. Mr. Solly Flood, a man who held several official positions in Gibraltar, and who was in charge of the investigation of the incident, suspected that somehow or other Captain Morehouse was responsible for whatever had happened to the *Mary Celeste*.

In the proceedings that were held before the Admiralty court Flood tried to sieze upon a few points to make a case that the captain and crew of the *Celeste* had been done away with by violence. There had been a brown stain on the deck that might have been blood. There was a cut in a railing that might have been made by a sword slash. The captain's sword, found under his berth, had a few spots on it that might also have been blood. But he was grasping at straws.

Flood made a more substantial point when he examined the final entry in the *Mary Celeste*'s log. It had placed the ship off Santa Maria Island on November 24, heading northeast. Eleven days later, according to the men of the *Dei Gratia*, she had been found 550 miles farther on than Santa Maria, and still heading northeast. How could a ship without a crew have drifted on course for so long? The implication was that the *Dei Gratia* had encountered the *Celeste* some days earlier than they reported and wished to hide that fact.

This point would have been an impressive one to those who knew little of the customs of the sea at the time. They would not have known that a ship's log was not kept daily. Captains generally made entries only when they had something of interest to report. Thus, it was perfectly possible for the crew of the *Mary Celeste* to have been on board for several days after November 24, without their captain having made any entry in the

34

log. The members of the court were aware of this practice, and were unimpressed by Flood's argument.

Flood's wildest shot came when he suggested that the crew of the *Mary Celeste* had drunk some of the alcohol on board and then, in a fit of drunken frenzy, murdered the captain, his wife and child, and the first mate. In order to escape prosecution for their murders they then abandoned ship, with the intention of telling any ship that rescued them that their own vessel had struck on rocks and the captain and mate had been killed.

It was quickly determined that the alcohol on board the *Mary Celeste* was of the commercial variety and quite undrinkable—indeed, quite deadly. While it was possible that for some other reason the crew had murdered Briggs and his family and thrown their bodies overboard, then abandoned ship themselves, there is not a shred of evidence to indicate that is what happened.

Captain Morehouse and the crew of the *Dei Gratia* were quickly cleared by the court. The members haggled a good deal longer over the financial arrangements. The final settlement was that the *Dei Gratia* and her crew got about one-fifth of the combined value of the salvaged ship and her cargo. That was less than they might have expected. But they also obtained, quite unknowingly, a measure of immortality.

The *Mary Celeste* was then turned back to her American owner, James Winchester.

The court was supposed to render an opinion as to the cause of the tragedy. During their investigation they had consulted everybody who could conceivably have been involved in the disappearance, or who might have some information or informed opinion about it. They queried every port within reach for news of possible survivors. All the naval experts, marine

Captain David Reed Morehouse, master of the Dei Gratia.

brokers, shipbuilders, meteorologists, criminologists, and zoologists who could be reached were asked for opinions. After three months of investigation the court was forced to admit that it hadn't the faintest idea what had happened to the *Mary Celeste*.

It was the first time in its history that the court had failed to come up with an opinion.

When the *Mary Celeste* returned to New York, Winchester sold her almost immediately. Over the next decade she changed owners frequently, finally winding up in the hands of a dishonest old sea dog named Gilman C. Parker. Parker's scheme was to fill the *Celeste* with worthless cargo, insure her for more than she was worth, then sink her for the insurance money. The *Celeste* met her end in the Haitian Gulf of Gonaïves in January, 1835. But the crime had been bungled, and the authorities found out about it. Captain Parker and three of his partners went on trial for barratry—a hanging offense in those days—and just barely escaped with their lives.

So ended the career of the *Mary Celeste*—but the mystery did not die with her. While the court of inquiry could offer no opinion as to what had happened to those aboard the *Mary Celeste*, that has not stopped a lot of others from offering opinions.

The theory that is mostly widely accepted by students of the mystery is the one first offered by James Winchester, owner of the *Mary Celeste*. The cargo was crude alcohol. Even though well stowed, some of it inevitably would have leaked after being shaken up in rough weather. One or perhaps more of the casks was damaged; evidence is not entirely clear on this point. The hot weather of the Azores would have turned the leaking alcohol to vapor. Enough pressure might have built up in the hold to blow open the hatch cover. One of the forward hatch covers was found open.

Though an experienced mariner, Captain Briggs had never carried a cargo of alcohol before. He may have seen what he thought to be smoke pouring out of the hold. Then there was an explosion, and he may have feared fire. His anxiety would doubtless have been increased by the presence of his wife and infant daughter on board. In a moment of panic he ordered the crew to abandon ship. The small boat into which they jumped could easily have been swamped and sunk, leaving the empty, but perfectly sound *Mary Celeste* to drift to its fateful meeting with the *Dei Gratia*.

Would an experienced seaman have panicked in such a way? The explosion of alcohol fumes could not have been a very large one, for no damage to the hold was found by investigators. Yet there are other cases in which ships were abandoned in a moment of unreasoning fear. It was suggested that Captain Briggs may have died of a sudden illness, or been swept overboard. Then, in the face of an emergency, panic would have been more likely. But wouldn't the death of a captain have been marked in the log?

Other theories have invoked pirates and elaborate conspiracies, often involving both the crew of the *Mary Celeste* and the *Dei Gratia*. One fairly recent theory that attracted attention, for its novelty if nothing else, suggested that the crew had eaten food contaminated with the ergot fungus, the fungus from which the hallucinogenic drug LSD is derived. The fungus itself is capable of causing hallucinations (as well as painful death), and as this theory runs, the captain and crew of the *Mary Celeste*, afflicted with horrifying hallucinations, dashed madly off in the yawl.

Others have suggested waterspouts, freak waves, submarine volcanic eruptions, even sea monsters as the cause of panic, though why anyone in his right mind would leave a ship for a small open boat when faced with these terrors escapes me.

Finally a host of "mysterious" forces have been invoked, and

Captain Benjamin Spooner Briggs, master of the Mary Celeste.

these have been anything from space and time "anomalies" to the presence of UFOs. No explanation has been really satisfying, and the *Mary Celeste* was, and remains, a true mysterious disappearance of the sea.

While most everyone would agree that the *Mary Celeste* is the most famous of the ghost ships, there would be considerable competition for the number two spot. But the *Carroll A. Deering* would surely come near the top of anyone's mystery list.

In the cold dawn light of January 31, 1921, watchmen at the Cape Hatteras (North Carolina) Coast Guard Station observed a large five-masted schooner rammed against Diamond Shoals along the Outer Banks. Seas were so rough that it was four full days before the Coast Guard could get a cutter close enough to the ship to identify and board her.

The ship turned out to be the *Carroll A. Deering* of Bath, Maine. She was named after the son of the man who had built her. She was entirely deserted except for two gray cats found in the galley. All the sails had been set, but the lifeboats were gone.

Unlike the *Mary Celeste*, the *Carroll A. Deering* was badly damaged and had run aground. The weather was terrible, and the Outer Banks were a well-known ship's graveyard. It seemed fairly obvious that the *Deering* had been abandoned when the crew found that she was in danger of sinking or breaking up. The crew in small boats might have perished in the storm anyway. Yet the more the case was investigated the more mysterious it became.

The *Deering* was on a return voyage from South America. Her captain was Willis B. Wormell, a sixty-six-year-old veteran ship's master who had been called out of retirement to replace the regular captain who had become ill on the outward voyage. While in Rio, Captain Wormell had met a friend, and confided to him his utter disgust with the ship's first and second mates, and the entire crew. Captain Wormell appeared to regard the whole lot, except engineer Herbert Bates, as worthless drunkards. In fact, the mate was arrested for drunkenness in Rio, and the captain had to make special arrangements for his release so that the *Deering* could sail.

The *Deering* left Rio for Barbados on December 2. It sailed from Barbados on January 9 for Norfolk. Early on the afternoon of January 23, 1921, she passed the Cape Fear, North Carolina, lightship. The lightship officers noticed nothing amiss about the ship.

On the night of January 27 a terrific storm hit the area, bringing winds up to 75 miles per hour. The storm calmed a bit by the twenty-ninth, and at 4:00 P.M. that day the *Deering* was sighted by the Cape Lookout lightship off Diamond Shoals. The distance between the Cape Fear and Cape Lookout lightships is about 35 miles. The *Deering* had taken six days to travel the distance, though the weather had been bad for only the final two days.

To the men of the Cape Lookout lightship it was clear that something was now very definitely amiss on the *Carroll A. Deering*. Captain Thomas Jacobson of the lightship saw that the whole crew was gathered on the quarterdeck. Normally only officers stood on the quarterdeck. To Captain Jacobson this indicated a lack of discipline on board.

One of the men of the *Deering* hailed the lightship through a megaphone: "We've lost both anchors while riding out the storm off Frying Pan [Cape Fear] Lightship. We want to have it reported ashore."

Captain Jacobson recalled that the man who was shouting the message had red hair, and spoke with a foreign accent. He didn't look or behave like a ship's officer. He certainly wasn't the aged Captain Wormell. Nor did the description fit that of any of the other officers, except possibly the boatswain, Johan

41

Frederickson. But one man, who had been acquainted with the officers and crew of the *Deering*, said that he could not remember a single redhead in the group.

The radio on the lightship had gone out during the storm, so the *Deering*'s message was not relayed ashore. As it turned out, that would have made no difference, for no one from among the twelve officers and crew of the *Carroll A. Deering* was ever seen again, alive or dead.

About an hour after the *Deering* passed the lightship, an unidentified motor-driven vessel passed, steaming in the same direction as the *Deering*. The men of the lightship tried to pass the *Deering*'s message on to the unknown ship, but she ignored repeated signals. The mystery ship has never been identified. Some have speculated that she was a pirate or a rumrunner—prohibition was still the law of the land at that time. Normally, though, ships of this type were careful to avoid the vicinity of lightships.

Another possibility is that the mystery ship was the *Hewitt*, a steamer out of Portland, Maine, which could easily fit the description. The *Hewitt* disappeared at about the same time and in the same area. But if it was the *Hewitt* that passed the lightship, why had she not responded to the signals? Unless, of course, she and the *Deering* were up to some dark and sinister doings.

Two mornings after the *Deering* was spotted by the lightship, she was found abandoned on Diamond Shoals, about fifty miles to the north.

The weather was bad, and it was not surprising that the *Deering* had foundered in the heavy seas. Two red lanterns, signals of distress, were hung in her rigging. Unlike the *Celeste*, she had been badly damaged, and was clearly unseaworthy. It would not have been strange for the crew to trust to the life-boats, rather than risk their necks on a ship that could no longer be controlled.

The crew of the *Celeste* had abandoned a perfectly sound ship in apparent panic, leaving behind practically everything. Investigation showed that the crew of the *Deering* had removed most of their luggage and clothing. The captain's large heavy trunk, grip, and canvas bag were also missing. It is unlikely, to say the very least, that the men of the *Deering* would have piled all of this bulky baggage into the small boats during an emergency evacuation.

One thing left aboard the ship was the chart. Captain Wormell had marked his course in pencil on the chart until January 23, when the ship was off Cape Fear. After that, another person began tracing the course for about a week before the vessel was found abandoned. Several pairs of boots, not belonging to the captain, were found in his cabin, indicating that others had been using the captain's cabin.

The mystery of the *Mary Celeste*, at least as far as the public at large was concerned, grew rather slowly. That may have been due in part to the slowness of communications in those days. The *Carroll A. Deering* mystery, on the other hand, almost immediately became headline news. In addition to the disappearance of the crew of the *Deering*, and the missing *Hewitt*, several other ships disappeared at approximately the same time. They probably sank in the unusually severe storms that were whipping the coast during the early months of 1921. But for many, such an explanation was too simple. In 1921 the United States was in the grip of an anticommunist hysteria, and the rumor got around that communist-influenced sailors were going to take over American ships and sail them to Russia or, alternately, that Russian pirates were seizing the ships. A front-page story in *The New York Times* of June 22, 1921, reported:

"The names of three other vessels which have disappeared off the Atlantic coast of the United States in mysterious circumstances were added by the Department of Commerce today to the list of those . . . more or less related to the supposed kidnapping of the crew of the American schooner *Carroll A. Deering* . . . it is not asserted that all the missing vessels were the victims of pirates or possibly Bolshevist sympathizers . . . but the fact that all these vessels disappeared at about the same time, and that none of them left a trace is considered significant. . . ."

The red or pirate kidnap theory seemed immeasurably strengthened on April 26, when a man named Christopher Columbus Gray reported he found a bottle with a note in it while walking on the beach of Buxton, North Carolina, a village near Cape Hatteras. The message read:

"*Deering* captured by oil-burning boat. Something like chaser taking off everything, handcuffing crew. Crew hiding all over ship. No chance to make escape. Finder please notify headquarters of *Deering*."

Naval authorities tend to be highly suspicious of notes found in bottles. But Captain Wormell's wife and daughter were energetic in pursuing the investigation. With the advice of several handwriting experts, they offered the opinion that the writing resembled that of Herbert Bates, the engineer on the *Deering*, and the only member of the crew that Captain Wormell was known to have trusted.

An examination of the notepaper, and of the bottle in which the note was found, determined that both could have been purchased in South America, from which the *Deering* was returning.

44

In September, however, the U.S. Departments of Commerce and Justice jointly announced that Gray had confessed that the note in the bottle was a hoax. This did not satisfy some of Captain Wormell's relatives, who believed that pressure had been brought to bear on Gray to make a false confession.

Charles Fort, an American writer who liked to collect odd data, found a whole string of ships that had disappeared at that time. Fort is still revered by those who see the world as being full of mysteries, and the fact that he had taken an interest in the *Carroll A. Deering* and allied disappearances has helped to perpetuate their fame. Fort offered no definite opinion as to what had happened—he rarely offered a definite opinion about anything. But he did note that the disappearances were mysterious and unexplainable.

The U.S. Weather Bureau tried to squelch the idea that there had been a whole rash of mysterious disappearances in January and February of 1921. Officials there pointed out that the North Atlantic had been unusually stormy. A spokesman for Lloyds of London, a firm with a long history of insuring ships, said that, considering the weather, the number of vessels reported missing was not exceptional.

Other insurance underwriters noted that at the time, the shipping business was depressed, and owners were losing money. During such a period sinkings tended to increase, either because owners deliberately had their ships sunk, or tended to take greater risks with their craft by sending them out poorly maintained.

It has often been suggested that at some point Captain Wormell had become ill, and was transferred at sea to another ship, which was later lost—the *Hewitt*, for example. This would partially explain the strange behavior of the *Deering* crew when they passed the Cape Lookout lightship. But if the captain was not on board at the time or was seriously ill, why did they not report that? The loss of a captain is much more important to a ship than the loss of an anchor.

Perhaps the entire crew transferred to another ship that was later lost. But why would the men have stopped to take their heavy baggage, and what had happened before the transfer? Another frequently mentioned theory is that there was a mutiny on board, or at least a fight, in which the captain was injured or killed. The crew may then have either abandoned ship and been swamped in the small boats, or been taken on by another ship which sank. A variation of this theme is that there was collusion between the crews of the *Deering* and some other ship like the *Hewitt* that was sunk. Perhaps the crews had conspired in a piracy scheme.

There are no firm answers to the many questions that have been raised concerning the fate of the captain and crew of the *Carroll A. Deering*. The more the case is investigated the stranger it becomes.

The *Deering* itself was declared unsalvageable, and a menace to navigation. It was dynamited, but the bow section washed ashore on Ocracoke Island in the Outer Banks. There it remained until swept back to sea during a hurricane in 1955.

The Pacific Ocean also has its share of mysterious disappearances. Perhaps the most celebrated in recent years concerns the 1955 disappearance of twenty-five persons, the passengers and crew of the motorship *Joyita*, in the vicinity of Western Samoa.

On October 3, 1955, the *Joyita* left Apia, Western Samoa, for the port of Fakaofo in the Tokelau Islands, 270 miles to the north. Under normal conditions the voyage would have required about forty hours.

When the ship failed to arrive as expected, an extensive air and sea search was launched, but no trace of the *Joyita* was found. It was assumed that she had become another of those ships that had sunk without a trace.

It wasn't until November 10, some thirty-eight days after the *Joyita* had disappeared, that the British colony ship *Tuvalu* sighted a derelict drifting helplessly some 450 miles west-southwest of the port from which the *Joyita* had departed. As the *Tuvalu* came closer to the badly damaged hulk, it became clear that the *Joyita* had finally been located. But that was only the beginning of the mystery.

The search was resumed, this time for possible survivors, but none was ever found. The *Joyita* was towed to port and an investigation of the events surrounding the disappearance of the twenty-five aboard was begun.

There was no lack of theories as to what had happened. One that popped up almost immediately was that the ship had been attacked by Japanese pirates who had murdered the crew and passengers and looted the ship. Less than a decade had passed since the end of World War II and the Japanese were still very unpopular in the islands.

Another theory was that an underwater volcanic explosion had thrown passengers and crew overboard. Just such an incident had taken place a few months earlier. The region in which the ship was found drifting was known for underwater explosions. However, none had been recorded in the vicinity at the time of the disappearance.

Other theories included freak waves or waterspouts that swept all aboard into the sea. Either was possible, but the idea that everybody, or even a majority of those aboard, would have been thrown into the sea at one time seemed highly improbable.

47

As the investigation into the disappearance of those aboard the *Joyita* proceeded, one thing became clear. The ship had been in very poor repair before it left port, and probably should never have been allowed to get underway in the first place.

Owner and captain of the ship was one Dusty Miller, a colorful island character, but one who had fallen on hard times. He lacked the money to maintain the *Joyita* properly. He evidently hoped to recoup his losses by using the *Joyita* to carry supplies and passengers to the Tokelau Islands, which did not have a regular ship service and badly needed supplies. The operation would have been very profitable, had Miller been able to get it going. But there was one delay after another, and in the few weeks before his last voyage, Miller had been reduced to living on his ship, and picking up odd jobs in order to get enough money to buy food. He confided to friends that he had sometimes gone several days with hardly anything to eat.

When Miller finally did get everything ready for his voyage and set out, there was an explosion in the engine room shortly after the *Joyita* left port. She began to drift helplessly, until an anchor was thrown out. She made it back to port where emergency repairs were hastily performed. The authorities were considering forbidding the *Joyita* permission to sail, but Captain Miller managed to get his ship in working order and away before they made up their minds.

After examining the *Joyita*, a commission of inquiry was able to establish certain facts. A pipe into the engine's salt-water cooling system had been badly corroded and burst, causing a serious and hard-to-locate leak. Water quickly knocked out the ship's electrical system, cutting off all power and leaving the *Joyita* to drift helplessly. All of this had probably happened just a few hours after she had left port. Even the emergency radio was not working properly, for investigators found a break in the antenna lead. Signals wouldn't have carried over two miles.

The ship was listing badly, and those aboard might have feared that she would sink. Part of the ship's superstructure had been torn away, perhaps before she was abandoned. Passengers and crew might have taken to the boats, only to be swallowed up by the sea a little later. But this theory runs into problems.

There is no dispute about the condition of the *Joyita*, the burst pipe or flooded electrical system. But no matter how badly damaged she may have been, the *Joyita* was virtually unsinkable, and Dusty Miller knew it. During her career the *Joyita* had been a refrigerated fishing ship, and her hold was lined with 640 cubic feet of cork. This meant that, no matter how badly damaged, she would float—well, like a cork. Miller had often boasted of his ship's unsinkability. That may have been one of the reasons that he set out on her, though he knew she was barely seaworthy. The fact that the *Joyita* was found floating over a month after she had been abandoned was eloquent testimony to her unsinkability. Why would Dusty Miller, or any sane person, for that matter, abandon an unsinkable ship, for the shark-infested waters of the Pacific?

There was no doubt that the ship had been abandoned. The boats, as well as the ship's log and navigational instruments, were missing. But it is also evident that someone stayed aboard. A piece of canvas awning had been lashed to a broken stanchion. The awning may have served to catch rainwater for drinking, shield someone from the sun, or both.

That raised other possibilities—mutiny, for example. The mystery of the *Joyita* made news around the world, but it was never really solved.

In 1962 a writer named Robin Maugham went to Fiji to

investigate the case for an article he was writing. He became so enmeshed with the mystery that he actually purchased the *Joyita*. After the tragedy the ship had been repaired, but quickly ran aground again. She got the reputation of being a "hoodoo ship," and was impossible to sell until Maugham came along.

During his investigation Maugham talked to a Commander Peter Plowman, one of those who had searched the empty ship after it had been hauled into port. Plowman had never been called to testify at the official inquiry because, after the burst pipe was discovered, officials felt that his testimony would not be necessary. While going over the ship Plowman had found a doctor's stethoscope, a scalpel, some needles and catgut for stitching, and four lengths of bloodstained bandages.

Maugham thought that this bit of information provided the last piece of evidence needed for a reconstruction of what occurred aboard the *Joyita* in October, 1955.

Shortly after leaving port, the ship ran into heavy seas, and the strain burst the pipe. The flooding which resulted stopped the engines and cut the power. The ship tried to radio for help, but the signals failed to carry, due to the break in the aerial lead.

The drifting ship was then hit by a large wave which tore away part of its superstructure, adding to the flooding, and to the panic of those aboard.

At some point while all this was going on, Dusty Miller was hurt, probably sustaining head injuries during a fall. He was treated by a doctor who was one of the passengers, but remained unconscious, and was unable to tell the others that no matter how badly damaged it might appear, his ship would not sink. This, Maugham deduces from the medical materials Plowman found.

The rest of the crew and the passengers, now convinced that the *Joyita* was about to go down, made for the boats, and were later lost in the rough seas. But someone had stayed behind, at least long enough to put up a canvas awning.

Maugham speculates that for some reason the injured Miller was not taken off the *Joyita*, and that one of the crew, probably Tanini, an islander who was devoted to him, stayed behind. Days or weeks later, another ship encountered the drifting *Joyita*. Miller was almost certainly dead by that time. Tanini may also have been dead, or the newcomers might have killed him and tossed his body and Miller's overboard. They looted what they could from the ship and left the *Joyita* to drift without a soul on board. If they had looted the ship, they would not have been likely to report ever having encountered it.

The explanation is an ingenious one, and it does cover the facts, so far as we know them. But, of necessity, it is made up of speculation piled upon speculation. A piece of bloodstained bandage does not prove that Dusty Miller was rendered unconscious. Chuck Simpson, another member of the crew, apparently also knew that the ship was cork-lined. Besides, he had already survived three shipwrecks during World War II. He certainly would not have panicked easily. Why did he abandon ship or allow others to? If some ship had actually encountered the *Joyita*, even to loot it, rumors would probably have gotten around. Yet there were none.

In any case, the disappearance of those aboard the *Joyita*, like the disappearances of those aboard the *Mary Celeste* and the *Carroll A. Deering*, have never been completely explained. They probably never can be completely explained, and so long as the smallest bit of doubt remains, they will continue to puzzle us, and perhaps frighten us a little.

51

4

Doors to Oblivion

It is difficult to imagine how anyone can have failed to hear of the Bermuda Triangle. In 1974 and 1975 the Bermuda Triangle was the subject of several best-selling books, popular magazine articles, and some televised documentaries.

Personally I was rather surprised by the sudden interest in the Bermuda Triangle. I had known about the Bermuda Triangle years before it became famous. It was one of the mysteries that those of us who are interested in odd things often argue about. The general public rarely even hears about such disputes. In fact, I knew about the Bermuda Triangle long before it became the Bermuda Triangle.

Just to refresh your memory a bit, the Bermuda Triangle is an area in the Caribbean where ships and planes are supposed to disappear mysteriously and regularly. The Triangle can be encompassed in an area bounded by a line drawn from Bermuda to Puerto Rico to Florida and back to Bermuda. That is a fairly considerable area, but when discussing the mystery of the Bermuda Triangle, many authors will include disappearances far outside it. The disappearances of the men of the *Carroll A. Deering*, for example, can be found listed among those mysteries somehow attributed to the Bermuda Triangle, though the *Deering* disappearances took place way up near Cape Hatteras in North Carolina. Even the *Mary Celeste*, which was found drifting on the other side of the Atlantic has, on occasion, been lumped in with the Bermuda Triangle.

But the most celebrated disappearance to take place within the Bermuda Triangle—and it really did happen in or near the Triangle—was the disappearance of a group of airplanes called Flight 19. In fact, it is a reasonable surmise that had there been no Flight 19 there would have been no mystery of the Bermuda Triangle. The flight's proposed route was triangular in shape.

The disappearance of Flight 19 has been called the greatest disappearance of the twentieth century, or the *Mary Celeste* of the air. We are going to examine it in more detail a bit later, but to trace the history of the idea of the Bermuda Triangle, we must at least sketch in the major details of the case here.

At 2:10 in the afternoon of December 5, 1945, five Avenger torpedo bombers took off from Fort Lauderdale Naval Air Station on a routine training mission. It was to cover a triangular route 160 miles straight east, north 40 miles, then directly back to base. Total estimated flying time was to be two hours. Four of the planes contained the full crew of three. The fifth contained only two men; one had failed to show up. When the planes took off the weather was good and there was no hint of trouble.

Within an hour and forty-five minutes, however, messages indicating that something was wrong were picked up from the flight leader. He said that his compass was not working, and he didn't know where he was or what the proper course was back

53

to the base. The messages from the flight were picked up at a variety of different ground stations, and they tried to help the flight leader determine position. It was all to no avail. Communications were poor and got worse, and after 7:00 P.M. no more communications were received from the missing flight. It was calculated that the planes had enough fuel to keep them in the air until about 8:00 P.M., and it was assumed that they ditched in the sea, though not a trace of wreckage was ever found.

When Air Force authorities realized that Flight 19 was in serious trouble they sent up search planes to try and locate the planes, or if they were down, to rescue survivors. One of the planes that set out was a Martin Mariner, equipped with full rescue gear. This plane, with thirteen crewmen aboard, failed

Five TBF Avenger torpedo bombers similar to those which disappeared over the Bermuda Triangle on December 5, 1945.

to report in at the scheduled time. It too was never seen again.

A full and exhaustive inquiry into both disappearances was held, but no final conclusions could be reached.

This most mysterious of mysterious disappearances within the Bermuda Triangle had taken place just after the close of World War II. What most account to be the second most mysterious disappearance occurred during World War I. On March 4, 1918, the USS *Cyclops*, a 19,600-ton Navy collier, sailed from Barbados, West Indies, with a crew of 309 men and a cargo of manganese ore. The ship, one of the largest afloat at the time, was bound for Norfolk, Virginia, but never arrived. Though the ship had a radio, no distress signals were ever received. Navy authorities assumed that the *Cyclops* was sunk somewhere in the vicinity of the Bermuda Triangle, but no wreckage was ever found, despite an intensive search.

German submarines were known to have been operating in the area at the time, and there was widespread suspicion that the ship had been torpedoed. But the Germans habitually broadcast news of the sinking of large Allied ships, for such events had immense propaganda value. No such announcement was made, though any U-boat captain would surely have accounted the *Cyclops* a prize. No record of such a sinking was ever found among the papers of the German war office. The torpedo theory can be discarded.

A whole host of other war-related explanations have been offered over the years. These have ranged from German sabotage to floating mines. For a variety of reasons none of the explanations has been very satisfactory.

The Navy genuinely regarded the disappearance of the *Cyclops* as a mystery of the sea. She was the first large radio-equipped ship to disappear without giving any radio warning,

The Cyclops, *which disappeared in 1918 with 309 men aboard.*

and she was the largest U.S. Navy ship ever to disappear without a trace.

An enormous number of other mysterious disappearances have been mentioned in connection with the Bermuda Triangle. Some of these are not very mysterious. In March, 1948, Al Snider, a well-known jockey, and two friends sailed out from Sandy Key, off Florida's southern tip, to do some fishing, and were never heard from again. What many of those who like to make mysteries fail to mention is that when the men were out fishing a gale struck the area. There is nothing particularly mysterious about a small boat sinking in a storm.

Two more romantic figures whose disappearances have been connected with the Bermuda Triangle are Joshua Slocum and Donald Crowhurst, both round-the-world solo sailors.

Captain Joshua Slocum was possibly the best mariner in the world around the turn of the century. He had sailed around the world in his 37-foot yawl, the *Spray*, and was the first man known to have done so single-handedly. Slocum was, by everyone's account, an absolutely magnificent sailor, who had accomplished feats that no other sailor could have.

On November 14, 1909, Slocum set out in the *Spray* from

Martha's Vineyard. His exact destination is unknown. Most think he was headed for South America, but some contend that he was planning a nonstop circumnavigation of the globe. In any event, he was sailing south, and was never seen again.

Devotees of the Bermuda Triangle mystery insist that Slocum disappeared in or near the deadly Triangle. This is possible, but by no means certain. Unconfirmed reports said that he was seen in a variety of different South American ports. In his book, *Mysterious Tales of the New England Coast*, Edward Rowe Snow, one of America's foremost experts on maritime mysteries, theorizes that Slocum's tiny craft was run down by a 500-ton mail steamer near Turtle Island, Lesser Antilles, while en route to the Orinoco River.

At the time of his last voyage, Slocum was in his mid-sixties and his health may have been failing. He is reported to have suffered from occasional blackout spells. He could have died of natural causes, or have fallen overboard during a blackout. Or he might just have been unlucky, and fallen victim to any one of the thousands of dangers that confront a lone sailor. Slower reflexes and waning strength would have made him more prone to accidents. Oddly, despite a lifetime spent at sea, Slocum could not swim—though swimming probably would have been little help had he fallen into the sea.

The disappearance of Joshua Slocum certainly ranks as a mysterious disappearance of the sea—in that we don't know what happened to the great mariner, and probably never will. But there is no reason to suspect that there was anything really unnatural about his disappearance, or even that he disappeared in the Bermuda Triangle.

The disappearance of Donald Crowhurst in 1969, which is also often mentioned in connection with the Bermuda Triangle,

Master mariner Joshua Slocum set off in his small boat, the Spray, *on November 14, 1909. He was bound for South America, but was never seen again.*

is, if anything, even stranger than the disappearance of Slocum, but it is not in the least mysterious—for we know exactly what happened.

Moreover, his trimaran (three-hulled craft) *Teignmouth Electron* was found floating, abandoned, 700 miles southwest of the Azores. That is roughly the area in which the *Mary Celeste* was found, but it is nowhere near the Bermuda Triangle. Still, some devotees of the Bermuda Triangle mystery profess to find a connection between the disappearance of Crowhurst and the Triangle.

At the time that Crowhurst's 41-foot, three-hulled yacht was found abandoned he was believed to be the leader in a solo round-the-world race sponsored by the Sunday *Times* of London. Reports received from Crowhurst indicated that he was leading in the race and was expected to dock in England in just a few days and collect his $12,000 prize as well as worldwide acclaim for having completed the fastest solo circumnavigation of the globe ever.

When the *Teignmouth Electron* was found, the London *Times* reported on July 11:

"There was no sign of the yachtsman nor anything to suggest what had happened to him. Books, papers, films and tapes, and Mr. Crowhurst's log were found intact . . .

"The yachtman's dinghy and emergency life raft were still on the trimaran . . ."

The mystery was soon solved when Crowhurst's books and papers were examined. Crowhurst had not been sailing around the world as he had claimed. On the contrary, he had spent eight months sailing aimlessly around the South Atlantic. He kept a false logbook, and reported phony positions by radio. At least one of the race's judges had already begun to suspect that there was something wrong with Crowhurst's reports.

Crowhurst would never have been able to maintain the fiction after returning to England. Perhaps he might have gotten away with the hoax, had he not been the leader in the race. He may not have originally intended to win the race, merely to finish among the leaders. But his reports showed him gaining so rapidly on the leader, Nigel Tetley, that Tetley pushed his boat too hard, and it broke apart and sank. That left Crowhurst a sure winner, and he could not stand the strain of the inevitable exposure that would follow.

His diary clearly recorded the mental breakup of Donald Crowhurst. The last entry in his logbook, written on July 1, was that at 20 minutes and 40 seconds past 11 o'clock in the morning he decided to "resign the game." Presumably he jumped overboard.

As I said, a strange story, even a spooky one, but there is no mystery—at least no mystery of the sea. What happened to Donald Crowhurst is a mystery of the human mind.

More on target and mysterious are two plane disappearances which added considerably to the lore of the Bermuda Triangle. These planes, the *Star Tiger* and the *Star Ariel*, disappeared, presumably as they crossed the Bermuda Triangle, though no wreckage was ever found.

The *Star Tiger*, a Tudor IV owned by British South American Airways, took off from Santa Maria in the Azores at 3:34 P.M. on January 29, 1948, and was scheduled to land in Bermuda at about 5:00 A.M. During the flight the plane regularly kept in radio contact with ground stations. The final message from the *Star Tiger* was received in Bermuda at approximately 3:00 A.M. The message was strictly routine. Yet the plane never landed.

An air and sea search conducted in the area in which the plane presumably went down failed to turn up any survivors, or indeed any indication that the plane had, in fact, gone down at all.

An inquiry into all aspects of the incident was conducted by the Ministry of Civil Aviation of Great Britain. The conclusions of the report have become rather famous in the annals of mysterious disappearances.

"In closing this Report it may truly be said that no more baffling problem has ever been presented for investigation. In the complete absence of any reliable evidence as to either the nature or the cause of the disaster to 'Star Tiger' the Court has not been able to do more than suggest possibilities, none of which reaches the level even of probability. Into all activities which involve the co-operation of man and machine two elements enter of very diverse character. There is the incalculable element of the human equation dependent upon imperfectly known factors; and there is the mechanical element subject to quite different laws. A breakdown may occur in either separately or both in conjunction. Or some external cause may overwhelm both man and machine. What happened in this case will never be known and the fate of 'Star Tiger' must forever remain an unsolved mystery."

And so it has.

That reference to "some external cause" created a wave of excitement among UFO buffs. They thought that the investigators had decided that the *Star Tiger* had been taken by a UFO, but were just afraid to say so. Actually, all the investigators meant by "external cause" was something like the weather. And, in fact, the weather was deteriorating at the time the *Star Tiger* presumably disappeared. It didn't seem bad enough to cause the plane to crash, but it was bad enough to create a rough sea and make successful ditching in the water difficult if not impossible. The poor weather would also have helped to scatter and sink any debris that might remain from the crash. It was many, many hours before rescue planes reached the area in which the plane was believed to have gone down and had enough light to conduct an adequate search. By that time the debris, if there was any, might well have been scattered and sunk.

If the disappearance of the *Star Tiger* were not enough, almost exactly one year later the *Star Ariel*, a sister ship to the *Star Tiger*, vanished in the same area under nearly identical circumstances. This time, however, the plane was only on a hop from Bermuda to Jamaica. The weather was excellent, and the only two messages received from the plane indicated that it was on course and there was no trouble.

Some confusion was evident when the plane failed to land as scheduled, and could not be raised on the radio. The confusion resulted in a delay in sending out searchers. When they finally did get out, no trace of the missing plane was found.

Once again a court of inquiry was held, and once again no reason for the disappearance could be given. There was nothing turned up in either inquiry to indicate that the cause of the loss of these two planes was due to some structural defect in the Tudor IV aircraft. They had been used successfully for a long time, and they were used again—to carry cargo. After the loss of the *Star Tiger* and the *Star Ariel*, Tudor IVs were never again used to carry passengers.

The idea of the Bermuda Triangle—that is, a special place where ships and planes disappear mysteriously—was apparently first born in 1964, in an article written for *Argosy* magazine by

Vincent Gaddis. After that, other writers have tried to hang different labels on the area—the Hoodoo Sea, the Devil's Triangle—but the term Bermuda Triangle is the one that has stuck.

Prior to the invention of the Bermuda Triangle idea, many of the disappearances had been discussed, but as individual cases. The disappearance of Flight 19 had been extensively written about for nearly twenty years. It was usually called "The Lost Patrol" and not necessarily linked to other disappearances.

The incident that seemed to have set Gaddis to thinking about the Bermuda Triangle was the 1963 disappearance of the *Marine Sulphur Queen* and her crew of thirty-nine. Disappearance isn't really the right word in this particular case, for the *Marine Sulphur Queen* most certainly sank. Pieces of wreckage were found. The mystery is *why* the ship sank.

The *Marine Sulphur Queen* was an enormous World War II

The Marine Sulphur Queen *vanished sometime after the morning of February 4, 1963.*

tanker that had been converted to carry molten sulphur. The cargo had to be kept at a temperature of 275° F. It left Beaumont, Texas, February 2, 1963, on a voyage to Norfolk. The tanker's path would have carried her around the tip of Florida and through the area of the Bermuda Triangle. She sent a routine radio call on the morning of February 4, and at the time her position was approximately 270 miles west of Key West. Attempts to contact the ship by radio after February 4 were unsuccessful, but it was another four days before any attempt was made to find the missing vessel.

Ultimately a few life jackets and other debris from the *Marine Sulphur Queen* were fished from the ocean in the vicinity of Key West. There was evidence that the life jackets had been used, but from the tears in the material it seemed obvious that the survivors had been attacked by sharks and probably torn from their jackets.

As with most of the other cases we have been discussing, there was an exhaustive but inconclusive inquiry held. In the case of the *Star Ariel* and the *Star Tiger*, there seemed no obvious reason why the planes might have gone down. With the *Marine Sulphur Queen* there were too many reasons.

Shortly after the ship's last transmission the weather in the area turned extremely bad. Ships of this general type have been known to capsize and/or break in two during storms. The profession of sailor is by no means a safe and easy one even today.

Then there was the cargo itself—15,260 tons of hot molten sulphur. The company which operated the *Marine Sulphur Queen* claimed, and still claims, that such a cargo is no more or less dangerous to transport than any other type of cargo. But we can't be sure, because liquid sulphur carriers were never common in the world, and since the disaster of the *Marine Sulphur*

Some of the debris from the Marine Sulphur Queen. *Life jackets were ripped, indicating that the survivors had been attacked by sharks.*

Queen they have become rarer still. While none has had a major accident in the last decade, we still don't have a great deal of background information to draw upon.

Ultimately the Coast Guard inquiry listed several possible reasons for the sinking of the *Marine Sulphur Queen*. The investigators just didn't pick a favorite.

Relatives of the missing seamen sued the company which owned the tanker, and for nearly ten years the cases wound their way slowly through the courts. In 1972 the Supreme Court let stand a lower court ruling that the ship was unseaworthy. Millions of dollars in claims have been filed, and the cases will probably still be going through the torturously slow court process for several more years.

So the *Marine Sulphur Queen* isn't really a very good mysterious disappearance. But it was a major tragedy, and at the time received a great deal of publicity. And it was the case that seemed to have gotten people seriously thinking that there might be something wrong with the area that we now call the

Bermuda Triangle. Actually, the tanker went down to the south and west of the Triangle proper, but no matter—it has become part of the story of the Bermuda Triangle.

There were no really spectacular disappearances in or around the Bermuda Triangle after that, certainly nothing to match Flight 19 or the *Cyclops* for strangeness. Of course, both ships and planes did "disappear"—that is, sink or crash in the region. That is hardly surprising; the area is heavily traversed by both ships and planes. Planes do crash, and ships do sink, for quite unmysterious reasons. But the area already had such a sinister reputation that the disappearance of any ship or plane anywhere near the Bermuda Triangle was immediately labeled as "mysterious."

The Bermuda Triangle seemed to grow tentacles, so that practically any disappearance like the not-so-mysterious disappearance of Donald Crowhurst became somehow linked to it.

In May of 1968 the nuclear-powered submarine *Scorpion* failed to arrive on schedule, and a massive search was launched to locate her and her ninety-nine-man crew. Five months later the shattered wreck of the *Scorpion* was located and photographed by the research ship *Mizar* 400 miles southwest of the Azores. The wreck lay in 10,000 feet of water, and chances of raising her are nil, so we will never know exactly what happened. In that sense only is the case mysterious. It is no disappearance. During her voyage the *Scorpion* had passed through the Bermuda Triangle, though she went down far from it, much nearer to Africa than Bermuda. Still, the *Scorpion* is often mentioned in connection with the Bermuda Triangle.

Interest in the Bermuda Triangle just continued to grow, until by 1974 it was probably the number one "mystery" in the United States, easily displacing such things as UFOs. Some people began to express a genuine concern about sailing or flying through the Bermuda Triangle, though there is no indication that any governmental body, airline, or shipping line has ever officially warned anybody about going through the area, or has taken the subject seriously in the slightest. From time to time United States authorities have warned of the dangers of the waters off Cuba, which lies just outside the Bermuda Triangle. While these dangers are strictly political, Triangle enthusiasts have eagerly, though incorrectly, seized upon the warnings as evidence that the government was closing the Bermuda Triangle to sea and air traffic.

All the publicity given to the Bermuda Triangle inevitably stimulated some critics to action. One of them was Lawrence David Kusche, a research librarian, who also had training as a pilot. Kusche had received so many requests for information on the Bermuda Triangle that he found that he had built up quite a file on it. After examining a lot of original documents on the various disappearances—investigation reports, contemporary newspaper accounts, and the like—he wrote a book called *The Bermuda Triangle Mystery Solved.*

Kusche's solution was that there really is no Bermuda Triangle "mystery." It is a legend, he says, created by people who either didn't know the facts, or chose to ignore some of them. Kusche is not able to provide an explanation for every single disappearance attributed to the Bermuda Triangle. Many of them, he says, are destined to remain unsolved for lack of information. But a lot of others are not mysterious at all, if one had troubled to learn the entire story. He does provide significant new insight into the two disappearances without which there would have been no Bermuda Triangle—the *Cyclops* and Flight 19.

In checking the weather reports for March, 1918, Kusche found that a severe storm had struck the area in which the *Cyclops* was located, shortly after her final radio message. In such a storm the ore-carrying ship could have capsized or broken apart so swiftly that crewmen never had a chance to radio a distress message.

There was no official inquiry into the disappearance of the *Cyclops* at the time. A war was going on and people had more immediate problems to worry about. Hence, the storm was overlooked and, as the tale of the disappearance of the *Cyclops* was retold, it was generally assumed that the weather had been good throughout the voyage, making the ship's disappearance seem more mysterious.

This mystery may really be solved one day, for in 1968 a Navy diver thought he located the wreck of the *Cyclops* on the sea bottom. The wreck was not marked at the time, and has not been relocated. But it lies within an area used by the Navy for diver training, and it may very well be found again. If it is indeed the *Cyclops*, we will at least know that it has not disappeared, and we may also learn more about why it sank.

In his reexamination of the case of Flight 19, Kusche did not come up with any new information, but by going over the testimony given at the official inquiry into the disappearance, he was able to draw some interesting conclusions.

Many strange statements have been attributed to the pilots of Flight 19. It has been said that they reported seeing a giant UFO just shortly before they disappeared, or that they suddenly found themselves over an utterly alien landscape. None of these statements appear in the official record of the inquiry. These statements have been suppressed, some might reply. Well, perhaps so, but where then did the writers of the books and articles on the Bermuda Triangle ever find out about them?

What the official record of transmissions from Flight 19 does show is that the pilots were lost and confused. The primary reason for this, says Kusche, is that the compasses in the flight leader's plane failed. He was unfamiliar with the area, and the other men on the flight were all trainees. In fact, when the flight leader first reported he was lost, he was actually on course.

The flight leader then failed to change his radio to the emergency channel, thus making communication between Flight 19 and the ground stations extremely difficult and unreliable. Still, at first, the situation did not seem terribly serious, either to the tower operators or to the men of Flight 19. The flight kept changing direction, assuming and hoping that they would reach land and be able to figure out where they were. All the time this was going on the weather, which had been fine when the flight took off, was getting worse and worse, and darkness was closing in.

By the time the seriousness of the situation was fully realized, it was too late, and the planes of Flight 19 were nearly out of fuel. Writes Kusche, "Flight 19 was not a group of experienced veterans touching down on a calm sea in the middle of a sunny afternoon—it was one disoriented instructor and four student pilots attempting to ditch at sea on a dark, stormy night. It was a hopeless situation."

There is even less mystery attached to the disappearance of the Martin Mariner sent out to search for Flight 19, says Kusche. What is often left unmentioned about this disappearance is that an explosion was seen by a ship, at the exact place and time where the plane should have been. Later an oil slick and bits of wreckage were sighted at the spot. It is assumed that the Martin Mariner exploded in mid-air.

What could have caused the explosion? Says Kusche, "Mariners were nicknamed 'flying gas tanks' because of the fumes that were often present, and a crewman sneaking a cigarette, or a spark from any source, could have caused the explosion."

In addition to the Bermuda Triangle, a number of other doors to oblivion—that is, places in which a large number of mysterious disappearances are supposed to have taken place—have been located by those interested in such things.

Next to the Triangle, the best known is the so-called Devil's Sea, a place about 250 miles southeast of the Japanese island of Honshu, between Iwo Jima and Marcos Island. This is an area of considerable underwater volcanic activity, and Japanese fishermen, who set out in small and frail boats, quite naturally regard it with some apprehension. But natural dangers aside, the Devil's Sea is also supposed to be a region in which a large number of mysterious disappearances take place. The late Ivan Sanderson, a collector of weird tales, took the subject a step farther by claiming that he had located about a dozen spots around the world into which planes flew and ships sailed—and disappeared with disconcerting regularity.

Walter Sullivan, science editor of *The New York Times*, had a little fun with all of this. He wrote a tongue-in-cheek column on what he called The Hatteras Hexagon. In the breathless style adopted by most writers on the Bermuda Triangle, Sullivan began:

"Among the perils of the deep there is hardly one that strikes more terror in the mariner's heart than the Hatteras Hexagon. His fear cannot be dismissed as seaman's superstition: Within this six-sided polygonal east of the Carolinas, no fewer than a thousand ships have vanished—in modern memory alone."

What Sullivan wrote was absolutely correct, and deliberately misleading. At least a thousand ships have disappeared—that is, sunk or run aground—in the Hatteras Hexagon. Some of these incidents are really mysterious, the best known being the mystery surrounding the fate of the crew of the *Carroll A. Deering*. For much of the year the region around Cape Hatteras is a stormy and dangerous place to sail. It has been known as a ship's graveyard for several hundred years because of its abundant natural hazards. Yet it is also on the main shipping lines which run up the East Coast of the United States, and an enormous number of ships regularly pass through it. Is the number of sinkings within the Hatteras Hexagon unusually high, considering the natural dangers of the area? Might it not be possible to construct a "mystery" like this around practically any well-traveled area of the sea's surface?

Sullivan continues:

"The record of the Hexagon, unhappy as it is, is but a chapter. The introduction to his authoritative 1952 atlas, F. L. Coffman, a specialist in marine disasters, cites the records of the United States Hydrographic Office. They show that an average of 2,172 ships each year went down, worldwide. Consider, he says, 450 years of world commerce, and the undocumented sinkings, and you can do your own multiplication."

Add to the ship sinkings the number of planes, large and small, that crash into the ocean, and it would not be overly difficult to compile an impressive disaster list for any part of the ocean.

This appears to be what has happened in the case of the Bermuda Triangle. The whole thing began innocently enough. There were a few good mysterious disappearances, particularly

Flight 19. Even today many would not regard that case as being solved. There have not been any new explanations offered for the disappearance of the two Tudor IVs.

But then, somehow, it all got out of hand. In order to make the mystery bigger and better, a variety of writers began to stuff everything into the Bermuda Triangle. Not only was the area of the Triangle stretched in order to encompass as many disappearances as possible, but all too often, significant information was just left out in order to make the story more exotic or thrilling. It worked—the public ate it up. Yet anyone truly interested in the strange and mysterious, not in the merely sensational, must have felt a bit distressed. I know that I did.

5

Vanishing Lands

Atlantis is, without a doubt, the most famous lost land in all of history. The story of Atlantis was first told by the Greek philosopher Plato back around 360 B.C. Plato said that he had received the information from a relative, who heard it from an Egyptian priest. In Plato's day it was assumed that Egypt was the oldest of all civilizations, and a repository of all ancient wisdom.

According to Plato, Atlantis had been a vast island continent located beyond the Pillars of Hercules, or what we now call the Strait of Gibraltar. That would have placed Atlantis somewhere out in the Atlantic Ocean. This land, said Plato, was the home of a great civilization. But the people had become cruel and arrogant, and the gods had destroyed them in a single terrible day and night. Atlantis sank beneath the waves, and everyone who had lived on it was drowned.

Plato had planned to say more about Atlantis, but the work in which he was to continue the story was left unfinished. We do not know why. Still, he told us quite a bit about the people,

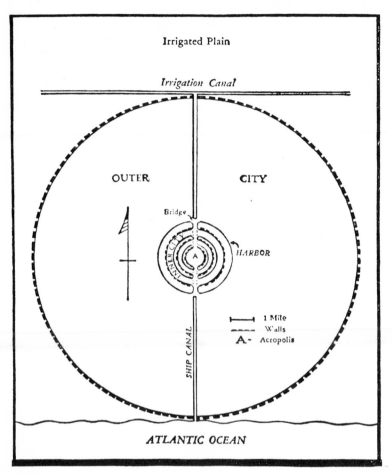

*The city of Atlantis as described by Plato. To the Greeks the circle was
the perfect figure.*

the government, history, economics, even the shape of Atlantis.
Plato is not only the best source for information on Atlantis, he
is the *only* original source, and it is important to remember
that.

There is no authority earlier than Plato, indeed no other
ancient authority who claims firsthand knowledge of the island

continent. They all refer back to Plato. Some ancients, including Plato's most celebrated pupil, Aristotle, doubted whether such a land had ever existed. Plato did sometimes make up stories in order to illustrate a point, and Atlantis might have been one of them.

Yet the idea of Atlantis has had an extraordinary hold on the popular imagination. In the more than 2,000 years since Plato wrote, millions—no, billions—more words have been written on the subject. Atlantis is probably more famous today than it was in Plato's time.

What's more, lost Atlantis has been "found"—dozens of times. It seems that every other year or so someone comes forth with a new tale of how they discovered the true location of Atlantis. Atlantis has been "found" everywhere from the North Sea to the middle of the Sahara Desert. Obviously all of these diverse identifications of Atlantis cannot be right—but they can all be wrong.

Just a couple of recent examples will give you an idea of how the search for Atlantis is generally carried out. Back in the late 1960s admirers of the American psychic and prophet, Edgar Cayce, decided that their hero psychically discovered Atlantis in the Caribbean near Bermuda. Some enthusiastic amateur scientists went skin diving in the place where they thought Cayce had located Atlantis, and found what they took to be the remains of ancient walls and pillars. This, they said, was clear evidence of the ancient sunken continent. More conventional authorities said that what they were looking at were barnacle-encrusted natural rock formations, which can look almost man-made in their regularity to the untrained eye.

But the Cayce enthusiasts had an even more spectacular bit of news—the seer had predicted that Atlantis would rise again, and that it would be fully visible, ancient walls and all, by the early 1970s. For several years Cayce supporters kept saying that Atlantis was rising off Bermuda. They produced aerial photographs which purported to show the dark land mass just beneath the surface. By now, Atlantis should be fully visible to all, but it isn't. Nor have the divers been able to produce any Atlantean artifacts from among their ancient underwater "walls." They haven't exactly given up on Cayce's prediction—but they have been rather quiet about it.

Undaunted by this failure, followers of another psychic set off on an expedition into the Atlantic off the coast of Africa in 1973. This psychic had, by some occult means, located Atlantis there. The expedition got a lot of publicity, and the psychic was absolutely sure of the location. So divers went down and found —nothing. But given the past history of the search for Atlantis, it will continue to be located in a similar manner for years to come.

There is, however, one location for the lost continent of Atlantis that is backed by quite a bit more than a psychic identification and a lot of wishful thinking. That location is the island of Thera.

Thera is a volcanic island in the Aegean located about halfway between the Greek mainland and the island of Crete. It is probably more accurate to say that Thera is the remains of a volcanic island, for about 3,500 years ago the volcano which built the island in the first place erupted in spectacular fashion. It may have been one of the largest volcanic eruptions of the past several thousand years. It certainly far surpassed any volcanic explosion to occur within historic times.

That such an explosion had taken place had been known by geologists for many years. Huge quantities of volcanic ash

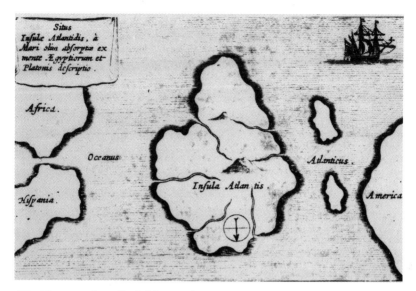

The "lost continent" of Atlantis, from a map printed in 1678.

blown out by the eruption had been found scattered over a wide area of the Aegean. But it was only during the 1960s, when investigators began to reexamine the area around Thera, that the Atlantis identification was seriously advanced.

As the explosion was reconstructed, it appeared that the volcanic island had once sat atop an underground cavern of lava. When the volcano blew, this cavern emptied out, causing a large section of the island to sink beneath the sea. This type of explosion is not unknown. A similar, though much smaller, explosion nearly destroyed the island of Krakatoa in 1883. The Krakatoa explosion is considered to be the most violent volcanic explosion of modern times.

Excavations on the remains of Thera revealed something even more intriguing. At the time of the explosion the island had been inhabited, by a highly civilized people called the Minoans. The center of Minoan civilization was on the island

77

of Crete, and the Minoans influenced the development of Greek civilization. Excavations are still being carried forward on Thera. It may one day be regarded as one of the great archaeological sites of the world, for volcanic eruptions often preserve more than they destroy.

Not only did the explosion destroy Thera, but there is speculation that it weakened, and ultimately brought about the decline of Minoan civilization. The theory runs thus: Tidal waves created by the explosion of the volcano wrecked Minoan ships and harbors—a severe blow, since the Minoans were primarily a sea-going people. The rain of volcanic ash, which fell heavily on Crete and neighboring islands, disrupted agriculture, another severe blow. The Minoans were never able to recover fully from these twin blows and ultimately fell to invading Greek barbarians from the north.

There are no surviving contemporary records of this catastrophe. The writing of the Minoans has not yet been deciphered. Even so, they did not appear to have done a great deal of writing, or at least not a great deal of it has survived. What we have will probably turn out to be ceremonial inscriptions and commercial accounts. There are no references to the explosion in the early Greek records, but much has been lost over the centuries. It is possible that Plato had heard of the explosion, and used it as a basis for his Atlantis tale.

The theory is plausible, but far from certain. There are a host of unanswered questions: Why did Plato move the scene of the disaster from the Aegean to the Atlantic? Why did he make Atlantis a continent, not an island? Why did he not mention its connection with the island of Crete, which was well known to him? And why did Plato place the date of the catastrophe some 7,000 years before his own time, when it was, in fact, little more than 1,000 years earlier? These are some of the problems. Plato may have received garbled information. He may have altered and exaggerated what he had been told, in order to make his story more dramatic. Or the explosion which destroyed part of Thera may have nothing whatever to do with the Atlantis story.

Even if the volcanic explosion in the Aegean did inspire the original Plato account, Thera is a small island. It is far, far removed from the idea of a "lost continent" which contained some sort of supercivilization. Until and unless much better evidence turns up to prove that there really was a mid-Atlantic continent that has sunk beneath the waves, it is reasonable to regard the "lost continent" of Atlantis as primarily a myth.

The mythical label can be pinned even more firmly on Lemuria and Mu, two names for a lost mid-Pacific continent. The evidence for such a continent is primarily the groups of tiny islands found scattered throughout the Pacific. These are said to be the mountaintops of Lemuria or Mu—all that remains above the waves of this drowned continent. The idea of a sunken continent in the Pacific is not an ancient one. It appears to have been born in the minds of modern occultists who wished to balance the lost Atlantic continent with one in the other ocean. Unless something much, much better in the way of evidence for the lost Pacific continent is forthcoming, it too must be regarded as purely mythical.

In addition to Atlantis and Lemuria, which have been much discussed, there are a whole host of lesser-known lands that have been believed in and reported in both oceans. Some of these places even appeared on maps drawn less than two centuries ago. Yet they can no longer be found.

Medieval tales speak of the lands of Ys and Lyonesse which,

like Atlantis, were submerged in a great catastrophe when the sea rushed over portions of the coast of Brittany in France and Cornwall in England. There is also considerable evidence that once-inhabited lands around the North Sea were submerged during some geological change thousands of years ago.

Before the peoples of the British Isles were converted to Christianity, they believed in a variety of wondrous islands out in the Atlantic. Judging from the fragments of ancient legends that have survived, these islands—which had such names as the Isle of Avalon and the Land of Youth—were sort of pagan heavens, equivalents of the more famous Valhalla of Germanic mythology. They were places where the spirits and perhaps the bodies of heroes went, after they died.

Stories concerning these wondrous isles were extraordinarily persistent. After the pagans were converted to Christianity, the islands themselves became Christianized, though rather incompletely. In legend the Isle of Avalon, a pagan heaven, became the place where King Arthur, a Christian hero, went to be cured of his wounds and to "sleep" until he was again needed to lead his people at some day in the future.

But surely the most intriguing Christianization of all of the legends of lost Atlantic islands are those which centered around the person of St. Brendan. According to tradition or legend, St. Brendan was a sixth-century Irish monk who made a long voyage out into the Atlantic, during which he had many adventures, finally landing on "The Fortunate Isles"—the island paradise which had so long haunted the imaginations of the Irish.

We don't really know when the first tales of St. Brendan's voyages were told. The first written version we have comes from the eleventh century, a full five hundred years after the saint is supposed to have made his voyage into the western ocean. But

80

the eleventh-century version is clearly based on much earlier accounts, now lost. Tales of St. Brendan's discoveries became widely known, and believed, throughout Europe. The earliest surviving version of the legend comes from France. There are those who believe that the tale influenced Prince Henry the Navigator, the Portuguese monarch who did so much to stimulate exploration, and that it had even impressed Christopher Columbus himself.

More recently there has been a great deal of speculation that St. Brendan had not discovered any magical islands, but rather, had discovered America. There has been some rather shaky evidence put forth to support the theory that there was a colony of Irish monks in New Hampshire hundreds of years before Columbus. But as far as hard facts are concerned, we have no idea what St. Brendan found—if he found anything at all—or if indeed there really *was* a St. Brendan in the first place. His voyages may simply be reworkings of older tales about pagan gods and heroes.

St. Brendan's islands are currently the best known of the phantom islands of the Atlantic, but there were many others. If you examine maps drawn in Europe between, say, the thirteenth century and the seventeenth century, or even later, you will find most of them dotted with islands that never were—or at least aren't there anymore. The most persistent of these islands was called Brazil or Hy-Brazil. The name may, or may not, have the same origin as the name of the South American country. That name comes from a red dye once imported from South America. But the island itself is something quite apart from the country. Some say that the name of the island originated with the Irish word *bres*, which means noble—the noble island.

81

Like many another uncertain Atlantic island, Brazil had a reputation of being a paradise, a land of the dead, the land of the setting sun, and so forth. It appeared on charts from 1320 to 1865 in a variety of places, everywhere from near the Azores to off the coast of Canada. At least one ship during the year 1791 reported seeing the elusive island at close quarters. Brazil had been given a variety of shapes, but was often shown as a perfect circle—which brings up an interesting point. Plato described Atlantis as being a perfect circle—the circle was the ideal figure to the Greeks. Is there any connection between the Brazil of the medieval maps and the Atlantis legend?

That question is an unanswerable one. Most authorities appear to believe that there is no direct connection between the two. Yet Greek ideas may well have filtered into Western Europe and, in a garbled sort of way, colored the beliefs of the people there.

Where did all these islands come from? In 1921 Albert A. Hopkins reviewed the subject of the legendary islands of the North Atlantic for the *Scientific American Monthly*. He concluded that these lost lands were almost certainly born in the imagination of the Celtic people who inhabited Ireland.

"The coast-dwellers saw the mirage or the cloud-bank brooding on the water; to them it was a floating island, possibly about to be disenchanted. They saw the foam spring high out to sea, and strange reflections below the waves; it was a magic land that lay there, and the gold-roofed towers and domes glinted deep under the waters, nay, it rose over the waters once in seven years, as men could attest. The ships of the Danaan and Sidh (demons and gods) sailed visible to all, reality and no mirage to the older tribes . . ."

Given the unsatisfactory nature of the evidence cited to

prove the existence of such islands, one is tempted to conclude, along with Hopkins, that they are indeed entirely imaginary. Yet even he was willing to admit the possibility that some lost documents may have described actual voyages to islands, which were later given a heavy overlay of mythology and folklore, so as to make the factual basis of the tales virtually unrecognizable. What makes the theory of a factual basis for some of these stories more attractive now than it was back in 1921 is that we have gained increased respect for the navigational feats of ancient peoples. It is now almost universally accepted that the Norsemen voyaged to America some five hundred years before Columbus. The voyages were recounted in Norse sagas, but it was assumed at one time that the sagas were entirely legendary. There is also increasing interest, though no firm confirmation, that any one of a number of other people, including the followers of St. Brendan, visited America even before the Norsemen got here.

It was once assumed that most ancient peoples were timid mariners, and that even the Greeks—renowned sailors of the ancient world—feared to venture far from the sight of land. But it is now recognized that a Greek mariner named Pythias, who lived in the second century B.C., made a voyage from southern France as far north as Iceland. This trip took him well within the Arctic Circle, and he gave the first recorded description of Arctic conditions, when he spoke of the "sleeping place of the Sun."

There is no serious doubt that Pythias actually did make such a voyage. Yet descriptions about the "sleeping place of the Sun" sound no less mythic than St. Brendan's islands.

The adventurous Swedish anthropologist, Thor Heyerdahl, has spent years attempting to show that the ancients could have

83

traversed both the Atlantic and the Pacific oceans in relatively simple craft. He crossed the Pacific in a balsa-wood raft called *Kon Tiki*, and later crossed the Atlantic in a reed boat called the *Ra*. Neither of Heyerdahl's successful attempts actually proves that such voyages took place, but they certainly prove that such voyages were physically possible.

Later peoples, most particularly the seafaring Phoenicians, are now thought to have made fairly extensive voyages. They went all around the African continent, and far out into the Atlantic, though how far no one is really sure. The Phoenicians were a notoriously secretive people. They were a trading nation, and if they discovered any new lands, they would not be anxious to alert possible competition. So we have few clear records of where they went and what they found.

Could they, or others like them, have sailed out into the ocean and found islands that are no longer there? And is it possible that memories of these lost islands were passed down in a garbled and fragmentary manner in some of the legends like those of St. Brendan and Hy-Brazil? That explanation has been put forth by a variety of unorthodox theorists. It has a seductively mysterious appeal to it. One wishes to believe it, and perhaps it is even true. But it is a mistake to lean too heavily on the evidence of the legends. We need more substantial support for the theory, and so far, such support is lacking.

Let's move from the mists of the ancient past to more modern times, where we have what are, or at least purport to be, first-hand, eyewitness accounts of islands that can no longer be found.

In this category we find the stories and/or legends concerning the Island of the Seven Cities, or Antilia, as it is often called. It

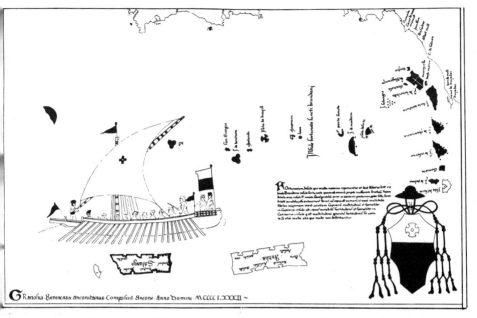

A map drawn in 1482 shows the Fortunate Islands of St. Brendan, Brazil, and Antilia.

was said that during the Moslem conquest of the Iberian peninsula (Spain and Portugal) in the eighth century, seven Christian bishops gathered their flocks and fled by boat to an island in the Atlantic. There they founded seven cities—hence, the name, Island of the Seven Cities.

In 1447 a Portuguese ship under the command of Captain Antonio Leone reported landing at an unknown volcanic island "where the people spoke the Portuguese tongue and asked if the Moors did yet trouble Spain."

Captain Leone said that he spent several weeks on the island. He found that it was divided into seven communities, each with its own "bishop" and a "cathedral" built of volcanic rock. Most intriguingly, he found that the people used large gold crucifixes and candlesticks and had altar cloths embroidered with gold

85

threads. Captain Leone said that his crew found that the sand on the island's beaches contained a high percentage of gold dust.

The Island of the Seven Cities was a regular feature of the maps of the fifteenth and sixteenth centuries. It was generally shown as a very large, rectangular island straight off the coast of Portugal—though the distance varied from map to map. The name Antilia means "island opposite." The existence of the Island of the Seven Cities was almost universally accepted, and on many of the charts the cities themselves were named—Asay, Ary, Vra, Jaysos, Marnlio, Ansuly, and Cyodne.

Columbus clearly believed in the existence of the Island of the Seven Cities, and he hoped to be able to use the island as a staging point for his longer voyage to the Indies. He expected to find the island in late September, 1492—but it wasn't there, and he had to sail all the way to America.

However, that did not end the search for this mysterious island. Albert Hopkins wrote, "England, having so narrowly lost her chance of being patron to Columbus, was now taking her place among the world-explorers. In August [1498] the minister of the Duke of Milan wrote to his master from England to say that [John] Cabot had found two large and fertile islands, San Juan and Prima Vista, and had found the 'Seven Cities' 400 leagues from England. Eleven months later the Spanish Ambassador in London wrote to Ferdinand and Isabella, telling of Cabot's discoveries and second expedition, and telling how 'the men of Bristol have for the last seven years [since 1492] sent every year, two, three or four caravels to search for the Isle of Brasil and the Seven Cities.' "

They didn't find either one and by the 1700s the name of the Island of the Seven Cities had begun to disappear from the

*A map made in 1492, the year Columbus sailed, still showed Antilia,
but not a hint of the continents of North and South America. The map
has been redrawn as a globe with the standard map-maker's grid.*

charts. In the meantime, in the New World the Spaniards were
searching for an equally elusive Seven Cities. These were supposed to be the center of a great Indian civilization like that of
the Incas, and like the cities of the Incas, the Seven Cities were
supposed to be filled with gold. These Seven Cities turned out

to be as elusive as the Island of the Seven Cities.

A rather curious controversy about the Island of the Seven Cities continues to this day. Some Portuguese historians contend that the story of the island began when a Portuguese mariner was blown across the Atlantic to Cuba, nearly a hundred years before Columbus set foot in the New World. He returned to Portugal and told his story to the authorities, who decided to hush the whole thing up, for fear that other countries would try and exploit the discovery. But word leaked out in a garbled way, and was elevated into the legend of the Island of the Seven Cities. However, aside from the Portuguese, who have a nationalistic interest in promoting the idea that one of their own discovered America before Columbus, who was in the pay of Spain, there is no one who takes the theory seriously.

Well, then, what is, or was, the Island of the Seven Cities? The orthodox explanation is that the island was entirely legenday. It has also been suggested that Portuguese refugees from the Moors may have landed on one of the Azores islands, and that this is how the legend began. There is a place in the Azores called Seven Cities, but there is no trace of an eighth-century Portuguese settlement, and the name itself may have come from the story rather than vice versa. Still, the theory is a possible one.

Then there is the least likely, and most sensational, explanation—there really was an Island of the Seven Cities, but sometime between the fifteenth century and the present day it has mysteriously disappeared.

This hardly exhausts all the tales of lost islands of the Atlantic, but let's look at the other side of the world. The Orient was not without its tales of fabulous islands that no one seems to be able to locate any more. The Chinese had legends of the "Isles of the Blessed," 700 miles eastward in the Yellow Sea. These were supposed to be places of ever-lasting spring. According to the tales, their secret was revealed to the Emperor Tshe Huan Ti about 219 B.C. Some sailors went out to find the islands, and saw them, but were unable to land because of a storm. Similar stories are told in Japan of the happy Isle of Oraison, far out to sea.

There is, unfortunately, not a great deal more that we can do with any of these stories from either East or West. They are very old, the evidence is fragmentary and inconclusive. We cannot be too hopeful that further investigation will turn up anything new. We can make of them what we will. But all the stories of disappearing islands do not come from the dim past— some, like that of Dougherty Island are comparatively recent.

The first sighting of what was to become Dougherty Island was made around the year 1800 by an American whaler, Captain Swain, of Nantucket. He saw what he took to be an island southwestward of Cape Horn. This would place it somewhere between the southern tip of South America and the Antarctic continent—an incredibly remote place in 1800, and not a well-traveled sea lane even today. Captain Swain described the island as being "covered with snow abounding with sea-dogs (seals) and fowl (sea birds)." Since the island was not marked on any charts, he named it Swain Island.

A few years later another Nantucket whaler, Captain Richard Macy, reported an island "four or five miles in extent" at about the same place that Captain Swain made his sighting. A confirming report also came from a Captain Gardiner of Sag Harbor. The reports all gave slightly different locations for the island, but this is not surprising. The calculations used by these

89

early nineteenth-century mariners to locate islands tended to be rough-and-ready.

In 1830 two American vessels made a concerted effort to find "Swain's Island." Records are incomplete, so we can't be sure how thorough a search they made—but, in any case, they could find no island and "Swain's Island" was gradually forgotten.

It wasn't until 1841 that Dougherty entered the scene. He was Captain Dougherty of the British whaler *James Stewart.* Dougherty's log for May 29, 1841, reports passing within a quarter mile of an unknown island five or six miles in length, and covered with ice and snow. Captain Dougherty admitted that the position he fixed for the island might be a little off, but not by more than a few miles. After that, the land sighted by Dougherty was called Dougherty Island, though since it was in the same region as the island sighted by Swain, they might well have been the same island. There were a couple of other sightings of Dougherty Island—but then it seemed to disappear from view once again.

Dougherty Island continued to be marked on the charts of the British Admiralty until 1935, though the last known sighting of the island took place in 1886. After that time a number of vessels passed around or over its charted position and saw no land at all. If Dougherty Island ever existed, it certainly doesn't any more.

Was this now lost island really a hoax or an illusion? Hoax can almost certainly be ruled out. There was no particular reason for a variety of sea captains to report a mythical island. Some of them were unaware that others had already reported an island in roughly the same place. An illusion—well, perhaps. Mariners had been fooled by mirages in the past. But most of the ships reported being too close to the island for the mirage idea to be plausible.

A far more probable theory was put forth by Rupert T. Gould, a British naval officer, expert on navigational instruments and collector of strange and mysterious tales. He says that the region in which Dougherty Island was said to lie was within the limit for icebergs emanating from the Antaractic. Gould continues:

"Now the Antarctic icebergs frequently attain a size which, at first sight, is apt to disconcert even experienced Arctic navigators. Flat-topped bergs five or six miles in length and rising several hundred of feet out of the water are by no means uncommon. . . . by the eye of a mariner not accustomed to Antarctic ice conditions, such a berg would be taken for an island far more often than not. And that a large berg should, in the absence of near-by land, be resorted to by numbers of seals is not in the least improbable.

"It seems not unlikely, then, what Swain, Macy, Dougherty, and the rest saw was a tabular iceberg; not of course the same berg in each case, but (so to speak) a standard pattern of berg, which they all met in much the same latitude because that was a likely parallel in which to encounter such a berg, and because it was about as far south as they cared to go."

Not unlikely, but not absolutely certain either—particularly when one considers the curious history of Bouvet Island, located in the remote and rarely traveled sea fifteen hundred miles southwestward of the Cape of Good Hope, the southern tip of Africa. "It is," Gould assures us, "the most isolated spot in the whole world—a fact which anyone who cares to spend an instructive five minutes with a pair of dividers and a good globe can easily verify. Around Bouvet Island, it is possible to draw a circle of one thousand miles radius (having an area of 3,146,000 square miles, or very nearly that of Europe) which contains no other land whatever. No other point of land on the earth's sur-

91

face has this peculiarity."

Despite its incredible remoteness, Bouvet Island was first discovered in 1739 by J. B. C. Bouvet de Lozier. He was looking for a southern polar continent. Antarctica hadn't been discovered yet, but most geographers assumed, for a variety of incorrect reasons, that there must be a Great Southern Continent. When Bouvet first saw the island that now bears his name he assumed it to be a part of that continent. The weather was too bad for him to attempt to land, or even get too close to the island, and he finally sailed away still convinced he had discovered the tip of the southern continent rather than an island about five miles in diameter.

Thirty-three years later the greatest of all navigators, Captain James Cook, twice tried to find the land located by Bouvet. He didn't find it. A colleague of Cook made another unsuccessful attempt to find the island. So, as far as the world at large was concerned, the land sighted by Bouvet simply did not exist.

Then, in 1808, Captain James Lindsay of the *Swan* not only spotted the island, but sailed right around it. He described it as being a small island surrounded by a great quantity of ice. The trouble was, very few believed him. Who was this unknown sailor to challenge the great Captain Cook?

During the next twenty years two other men claimed to have not only seen but actually landed on the island. Unfortunately, one of them was an American seal hunter named Morrell, who had picked up quite a reputation as a boastful liar. He wrote a book of his own exploits, filled with so much bombast that he made even truthful events sound unreal. One Antarctic explorer commented, "Reading Morrell, you have a feeling that if he came down and told you it was raining buckets you would be quite safe in leaving your oilskin below." But this time he happened to be telling the truth.

Bouvet Island kept being rediscovered, and lost, for another century. So little credit was given to its existence that it was on no charts, and very few mariners had ever even heard of it. So, on December 1, 1927, when a Norwegian whaler landed on the island, the captain hoisted the Norwegian flag there, under the impression that the island had never been discovered. In fact, it had been discovered 188 years previously and sighted or visited repeatedly since that time.

So the "lost" island of Bouvet was finally found—and it has remained "found." But what of the others?—and there are many in addition to those whose curious histories we have looked at here. Are they legendary or merely misplaced? With the oceans being mapped by ships with sophisticated electronic gear, by airplanes and by earth satellites, it seems impossible to conceive that we could overlook even the tiniest and most remote of islands. Yet people were once sure that Captain Cook couldn't make a mistake either.

6

Heavenly Disappearances

Perhaps you have heard of the planet Vulcan. If you have, it is probably as the home planet of Mr. Spock, the pointy-eared character from the televised science-fiction series *Star Trek*. But do you know that there really *was* a planet Vulcan? Or perhaps there wasn't but a lot of people thought that there was. It is an odd story.

On March 26, 1859, a French doctor and amateur astronomer named Lescarbault was studying the sun through his telescope. He saw a round black spot moving across the upper part of the sun's face. In his opinion it could only be a planet in transit, that is, a planet moving across the face of the sun. But which planet? All the known planets were accounted for; therefore, this black spot could only represent an unknown planet.

A few rough calculations—for Lescarbault was not much of a mathematician—convinced him that this unknown planet was a tiny one, with an orbit inside that of the planet Mercury. Mercury was thought to be the planet closest to the sun.

Lescarbault wrote up his observations in a letter and sent it off to Urbain J. J. Leverrier, Director of the Observatory of Paris. Not only was Leverrier the most distinguished astronomer in France, he had also been a participant in the discovery of the previously unobserved planet that was given the name Neptune. The planet Pluto, the outermost known planet in the solar system, was not discovered until 1930.

Aside from his undoubted scientific credentials, there was an unfortunate side to M. Leverrier's personality. He had the reputation of being the most disagreeable character in the French scientific community, perhaps in all France or even in all the world. When he received the doctor's letter in late 1859 he was furious. Who was this upstart to make such an important discovery? And why had he waited so long before informing Leverrier?

Leverrier went storming down to the doctor's office in the town of Orgeres, convinced that he was about to expose a fraud, or in the very least, a fool.

What he found was something quite different. The doctor was a pleasant mild-mannered man, who took no offense at all at Leverrier's rudeness, and answered all his questions with straightforward honesty. The doctor's astronomical equipment was poor, and his calculations primitive, but there was a distinct ring of truth about his entire story. All inquiries about the doctor's private character turned up highly favorable reports. Leverrier became convinced that the doctor had indeed discovered a new planet, because he had been lucky enough to be looking in the right place at the right time.

Actually, Leverrier and other scientists had long suspected the existence of such a planet. Astronomers had observed that there was something wrong with the orbit of Mercury. The planet did not behave exactly as theory predicted that it would.

The irregularity was slight, but astronomy is a precise and mathematical science—even small irregularities are extremely upsetting. It was as if two plus two kept coming out as 3.99999. Astronomers had suspected that the reason for the irregularity was that there was a small and unobserved planet within the orbit of Mercury which was disturbing its rotation.

This same irregularity in the orbit of Mercury, incidentally, remained a puzzle until the twentieth century. It attracted the attention of the young Albert Einstein, who managed finally to solve the problem in terms of his theory of relativity. However, an Einsteinian view of the universe was totally unsuspected in the middle of the nineteenth century. Unknown planets seemed a reasonable conjecture.

Upon Leverrier's urging, the village doctor was presented with the Legion of Honor, the highest award that can be bestowed by the government of France. Leverrier also calculated when Vulcan, as he named the new planet, should again transit the sun, and he asked observers in other parts of the world to try and spot it. But his calculations also indicated that the new planet would be so tiny that it might remain unseen, even to the most careful observer using the best equipment available at that time.

The existence of Vulcan did not go unchallenged. One observer said that he had been looking at the same spot, at the exact time Lescarbault had seen Vulcan. He was using a more powerful telescope, but still saw nothing. Yet, in general, astronomers accepted the existence of Vulcan, and kept careful watch at those times when it was supposed to pass across the face of the sun and become visible.

Several other observers did report seeing Vulcan, but they were the rankest of amateurs. More experienced observers could not confirm these sightings. However, two highly competent American astronomers reported locating no less than three tiny bodies orbiting the sun inside the orbit of Mercury. None of these bodies, unfortunately, could be identified with the elusive Vulcan.

Without firm confirmation, Vulcan gradually began to slip out of the realm of astronomy and into the realm of fiction and the occult. An American weather prophet named Tyce used Vulcan as part of the calculations by which he arrived at his not very accurate predictions. He also said he had seen the planet, but very few took that claim seriously because, as it was quickly pointed out, the time that Tyce reported seeing Vulcan, it would have been on the other side of the sun, had it existed at all.

Edgar Wallace, a popular novelist and dramatist of the early twentieth century, picked up, or perhaps independently arrived at, the idea of a planet on the other side of the sun. He wrote a serial called *Planetoid 127*, which concerned a planet that was an exact duplicate of the earth, which revolved in exactly the same orbit and at the same speed. This planet, however, was diametrically opposite our own Earth, and thus is rendered invisible from the surface of our planet.

It is interesting how ideas of this kind often enter the public consciousness as fact, and seem to go on forever. Quite recently I have seen the theory of the planet on the other side of the sun proposed very seriously by UFO buffs. They say that this mysteriously invisible planet is the place where all the UFOs come from. Few, if any, who put forth this theory know where the idea of a planet behind the sun originally came from.

So Vulcan probably never existed at all. But a question remains—what had Lescarbault seen? Most people assume that

97

he was an honest man, honestly reporting what he saw. What has been questioned is his ability as an observer. In 1891 the same Lescarbault announced that he had discovered a new and brilliant star. It turned out that he was looking at the planet Saturn. That is the sort of an error that even an amateur is not supposed to make. The best guess is that when Lescarbault thought he had seen Vulcan, he had observed a sun spot—a natural feature of the sun—moving across its face. Sun spots are generally irregular in shape, and thus readily identifiable, even to poor observers. Perhaps the one Lescarbault had seen was unusually round in shape, and looked more like a planet. We shall probably never know.

The disappointing deflation of the planet Vulcan does not mean that lost bodies do not orbit in our solar system. You may recall that while searching for Vulcan two American astronomers reported discovering three entirely different bodies orbiting inside the orbit of the planet Mercury. One of these astronomers, J. C. Watson, somewhat humorously endowed a Home for Lost Planets. During his career Watson had found twenty-two minor planets, or asteroids, and he wanted to make sure that their orbits were well tracked.

There are a huge number of asteroids—that is, large pieces of iron or rock orbiting in our solar system. The vast majority of these are in the asteroid belt, located between the orbits of Mars and Jupiter. The largest object in the asteroid belt is Ceres, which has a diameter of 480 miles. Pallas has a diameter of 300 miles, and from there on down, there are millions upon millions of chunks the size of basketballs, and innumerable far smaller pieces. It is assumed that the asteroid belt is what remains of a planet that broke apart at some time in the distant past. An alternate explanation is that the asteroid belt is a planet that never quite got together, for in theory all the planets were formed from swirling clouds of cosmic dust. Whatever the origin, the very large asteroids in the asteroid belt are well charted. Their orbits are known, and they can be located at any time.

There are, however, an unknown number of renegade asteroids. These asteroids have either broken out of the asteroid belt, or were never part of it. They orbit the sun in an irregular fashion, and their orbits cut across those of other planets, including the earth. That is what makes them so interesting, and more than a bit frightening. There is a possibility—admittedly a far outside one, but a possibility nonetheless—that one of these asteroids might strike the earth. The damage that a really large asteroid—say, one a hundred miles or so in diameter—might do is truly awesome to contemplate. Such a collision might, in fact, bring the world to an end.

Even a collision with a relatively small asteroid could be disastrous, particularly if it hit in a populated area. Some asteroids are known to pass close—that is, within a few hundred thousand miles of the earth—and yet astronomers have not been able to keep track of most of these asteroids. Now that may seem an extraordinary statement. We can keep track of a tiny satellite to Mars and beyond, yet we cannot locate a mile-wide chunk of iron that is, astronomically speaking, right in our own back yard.

Yet the statement is not as surprising as all that. Asteroids do not send out radio signals as do satellites, nor do they glow like comets. In the vastness of space an asteroid a mile or two in diameter is very hard to spot with a telescope. And by the time it is located it is often moving so quickly across the field of

Model showing the comparative size of the asteroid Hermes and New York City. Hermes passed close to the earth in 1937, but no one knows where it is today.

vision that it is impossible to obtain enough data on it to calculate properly its orbit.

In 1968 a mile-wide asteroid called Icarus caused a modest, though unjustified, disaster scare when it passed in the vicinity of the earth. The orbit of Icarus is known to astronomers. It was calculated that only a relatively small change in orbit would place the asteroid and the earth in the same spot at the same time. No scientist seriously expected this to happen, but even thinking about the possibility frightened a lot of people.

What most people did not realize is that in the 1930s three large asteroids passed even closer to the earth. The asteroid Apollo came within two million miles of earth in 1932. Adonis was within a million miles in 1936. In 1937 there was some genuine concern among astronomers when Hermes skimmed within a mere 485,000 miles of earth on October 30. That was still twice as far away as the moon, but it was the closest known approach of an asteroid to earth.

Where are Apollo, Adonis, and Hermes now? No one knows. As far as astronomers are concerned, they are "lost." Dr. Robert S. Richardson, formerly of the Mount Wilson Observatory in California, is one of those astronomers who worries out loud about even the remote possibility of an asteroid striking the earth. He has written:

"We are aware of these close-approaching asteroids only through the accident of discovery. No one knows how many objects ranging in size from a few miles in diameter downward may pass near the earth each year without being noticed."

There are several places on earth where scientists believe they have found the scars left by ancient collisions between the earth and an asteroid. Erosion and mountain building has tended to obscure the evidence, but some of the suspect places indicate that the impacts formed craters up to 30 miles in diameter!

Icarus, Hermes, Apollo, and Adonis all had diameters of about a mile. The largest asteroid to pass in the vicinity of the earth is Eros, which is fifteen miles in diameter. It caused a stir by coming close to the earth in 1898, but it is so large that astronomers are able to keep track of it.

You can see that there are a lot of things that get "lost in space." But unquestionably the most curious thing ever to get lost in space are the canals of Mars.

The close-up pictures of the Martian surface that were sent

101

back by the various Mariner space probes should have settled the question once and for all—the Martian canals didn't get lost because there really were no canals. But the question has been "settled" before, and it probably won't be finally settled until men land on Mars for a firsthand look.

How did it begin, this idea that Mars was crisscrossed with canals? The idea began in 1877 with the Italian astronomer, G. V. Schiaparelli of Milan. While observing Mars he saw some streaks on the face of the planet that had not been charted by any previous observer. This was not the first time Mars had been observed through a telescope—far from it. How was it, then, that other observers, with better equipment, had failed to notice the streaks?

Schiaparelli was viewing the planet at an exceptionally favorable time. At this same time the moons of Mars were first discovered. As the history of the planet Vulcan shows, astronomical observation was something less than an exact science. A lot depended—and still depends—upon luck.

Schiaparelli called the streaks *canali*, which really means channels—a neutral word that does not imply an artificial origin. However, the word was translated into English as canals, which certainly does imply an artificial origin.

The canals of Mars were not accepted at once, but then other astronomers began to see them as well. Astronomers of good repute almost seemed to be vying with one another as to the extent of the network of canals they could see.

But far and away the most influential figure in the entire Martian canal controversy was the American astronomer, Percival Lowell. Lowell was director of the observatory at Flagstaff, Arizona, at the time one of the finest in the world. Through his telescope Lowell thought he saw a whole spider's web of rigidly

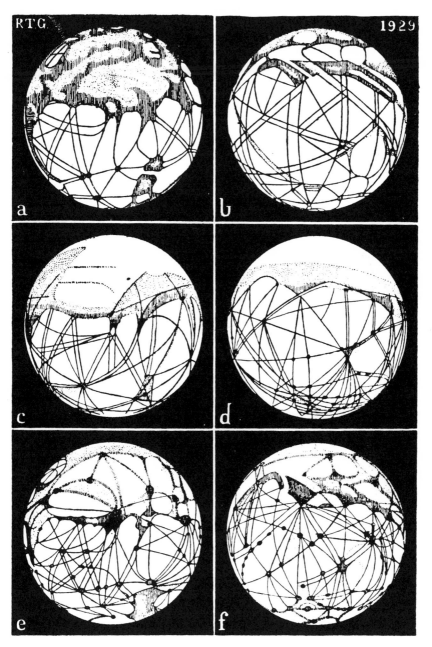

The canals of Mars as mapped by various observers.

geometrical canals. At the points where one canal intersected another he saw a circular dark spot, which he termed an oasis.

Lowell argued that the canals were of artificial origin, and that they had been constructed by the Martians in order to irrigate their essentially dry planet with water that came from melting polar icecaps.

Lowell's theories aroused a great deal of opposition within the scientific community. But until his death in 1916, Lowell stuck to his guns, and his disciples and admirers carried on after him, mapping the canals of Mars. They even claimed to have been able to photograph the canals, though persons less convinced of the existence of canals could see nothing on the photographs. In the end, earthbound photography could prove nothing, for the observer's eye was always more sensitive than the camera.

After Lowell's death the heat of the Martian canal controversy cooled down a bit, as fewer and fewer observers reported seeing the canals. But the idea of canals on Mars certainly did not die out entirely, for a small but not insignificant number of observers continued to see them. I recall hearing the late Willy Ley, one of America's leading science writers, describe how he had seen the canals while gazing through a telescope. He had been looking at Mars through a telescope off and on for many years, and had never seen the canals before. Then one day when the conditions were just right—there they were. He was convinced that those who had failed to see the canals just hadn't been observing under the proper conditions. He did not accept the idea that the canals were of artificial origin, but he was sure that Mars was marked with a network of more or less straight lines. Ley was not a professional astronomer, but he had a tough and skeptical mind, and was well aware of the long

Percival Lowell

controversy surrounding the canals of Mars. He was a man whose testimony had to be taken seriously.

Yet when the Mariner photographs of Mars were sent back, they showed the surface of the planet cratered like the surface of the moon. There were no oases, no canals, no signs of a high civilization. However, the photographs did show what appeared to be irregular water-cut channels, like dry riverbeds. This was an indication that at one time water may have been abundant on the Martian surface. Some of the photographs also showed faint straight lines. These are far too faint to account for the

Martian canals, but no one knows what the lines might be. Astronomer Carl Sagan has termed them "a real Martian mystery."

Whether Mars contains life is still an open question, though most scientists tend to doubt that it does. If it does, the life is probably microscopic, and of a low order. There is virtually no active hope at all that the planet contains intelligent life, much less life capable of digging a planetary network of canals.

What, then, are the "canals" that so many people had seen for so long? No one really knows for sure, and there probably is no single answer. Basically, it is felt that the canals were the result of an optical illusion—the tendency of the eye to link up various disparate features. The eye is far from the perfect instrument for recording reality, as a look at any collection of optical illusions will quickly demonstrate. Even the most passionate defenders of the canal idea admitted that the lines were faint. And perhaps, once the idea was planted in an observer's head that there were canals, by straining hard enough he was able to see them, even when they weren't there.

There is one more Martian mystery, though it is more in the nature of a mysterious appearance than a disappearance. I mentioned earlier that in the same year in which Schiaparelli "discovered" the canals of Mars, moons of Mars were also discovered. These were quite real, but there were some odd things about them. They are tiny, far smaller than most normal planetary satellites in the solar system. Their orbits are surprisingly circular. They are much closer to the surface of the planet than calculations indicate they should be. And they should have been discovered earlier.

One of the most frequently mentioned mysteries about the

satellites of Mars is how their discovery was predicted in 1726 by the English writer Jonathan Swift, in the book we call *Gulliver's Travels*. Swift had an episode in which he described how the people of the island of Laputa had discovered the satellites, and he gave a reasonably good description of their size and rotational period, though there was no concrete knowledge at the time Swift wrote that such satellites even existed. Swift's prediction has often been cited as one of the luckiest guesses in the history of science. More daring souls have hinted that Swift might have had some sort of "psychic" knowledge of the moon of Mars.

Perhaps so, but there is a more mundane explanation. In 1752 the French writer Voltaire also wrote about two moons for Mars. This was later than Swift, but still more than a century before the moons were actually seen. Voltaire said he had arrived at the figure of two moons "by analogy." The inner planets, Mercury and Venus, had no satellites. Earth had one. The planets beyond Mars had numerous satellites—therefore, Mars should have two, at least. Presumably Swift had reasoned the same way, but it was still a pretty lucky shot.

In 1862 conditions for viewing Mars were exceptionally favorable. Astronomers suspected that the planet had satellites, and were looking for them, but didn't find them. It wasn't until 1877 that the two moons were actually seen by Asaph Hall of the Naval Observatory in Washington. He saw them under less favorable conditions, and with a smaller telescope than had been available in 1862. The canals of Mars had also been missed in 1862, but as we now know there are no canals on Mars. Why had the moons of Mars been missed?

There are certain peculiarities about the size and rotation of the two moons that make them look more like artificial satellites than natural ones. One prominent Soviet astronomer, I. S. Shklovsky, proposed the "fantastic idea" that they really were artificial satellites put up by a long dead Martian civilization.

Then an American scientist, Frank Salisbury, came up with an even more fantastic idea. In the journal *Science* he wrote: "Should we attribute the failure of 1862 to imperfections in the existing telescopes, or may we imagine that the satellites were launched into orbit between 1862 and 1877?"

That is, by any reckoning, a very far-out possibility. But the nagging little question won't be solved conclusively until we get a much closer look at the moons of Mars than we have been able to manage so far.

7

Lost Secrets

It is both astonishing and depressing to contemplate just how much of the knowledge of the past has been lost, and that the percentage of the fragments that have survived has done so by the merest of accidents.

In the early years of this century there occurred a disastrous fire in the palace of the Sultan of the Ottoman Empire, in Constantinople. After the fire, crowds of looters invaded the building, and the police seemed powerless to stop them. A young diplomat working in the French embassy had gone to the palace in order to watch the excitement. The Frenchman noticed that one of the looters was carrying a very large and very old book from the palace. Being interested in books, he stopped the man and asked if he could look at it. The looter, apparently believing that he had a buyer for his stolen treasure, obliged.

The book turned out to be a complete copy of the history of Rome, written by Titus Livius, better known as Livy, who lived in the first century A.D. It was well known that Livy had written a massive history of Rome, so huge that it had reportedly been divided into 142 sections. Of these, only 35 survive, though something of the rest is known through excerpts used by other writers. But the recovery of any of the lost portions of Livy's history would have constituted an immense, almost unbelievable, historical treasure. And the treasure seemed to be in the possession of an unknown Turkish looter.

The French secretary offered the man a goodly sum of money for the book, and the Turk agreed. Unfortunately, the Frenchman was only carrying a few coins with him at the moment. He asked the Turk to accompany him to his residence where he would obtain the balance. Once again the Turk agreed. At that moment the mob surged forward, and the two men were separated. The Frenchman never saw the Turkish looter again, nor has any more ever been heard of the copy of Livy's history of Rome.

This story may be exaggerated, or it may be entirely apocryphal. We have no way of really knowing. But it is surely no stranger than the mystery surrounding the disappearance of the bones of Peking man. One might argue that bones are not secrets, or that since casts of the missing bones do exist, there is nothing new to be learned from them, and that their disappearance is really only a matter of minor importance. But this is most certainly not the case. Harry L. Shapiro, Chairman Emeritus of the Department of Anthropology at the American Museum of Natural History, has pointed out that a reexamination of other original fossil material has led to an entirely different view of that fossil's place in evolutionary history. A reexamination of the original Peking man fossils might do the same, especially since so much has been learned about the evolution of man since these bones were first found—and then lost.

The bones were unearthed in China in an old limestone pit

The limestone cave in which the bones of Peking man were first discovered.

near the city of Peking in the late 1920s and early 1930s. All told, the fossils appeared to represent fragments of some thirty early ancestors of man. It was a fossil find of absolutely unprecedented richness—for most fossil men and near men are represented by only a fragment of a skull, a few teeth, or at most, the partial remains of just a handful of individuals. Nothing quite like the fossil cache of Peking man bones had ever been found before. Nothing like it has been found since. The word "priceless" has been debased by overuse, but surely the word has never been more appropriately applied than to these utterly unique and irreplaceable relics of man's distant past.

The bones were discovered at the wrong time and in the wrong place. Political conditions in China in the 1930s were unsettled, but for a while the political turmoil did not touch the work at the site of the Peking man discovery.

By 1941, however, conditions had grown ominous indeed. Many of those who were working at the site were Americans, and though war had not yet actually broken out between America and Japan, relations were very strained. It seemed only a matter of time—and not much time either—before the Japanese would move to take over the site and the fossils. It was decided that the bones should be sent to America for safekeeping. They were packed in two ordinary footlockers, and were to be transferred to the care of the U.S. Marines near Peking, then shipped to the United States aboard the USS *President Harrison* that was waiting to evacuate the marines. At about this point the story gets a bit confused, for the *President Harrison* never reached port, and many of the American personnel were captured and interned by the Japanese. The two lockers containing the bones were never heard of again.

The most obvious, and most heartbreaking, explanation for

the disappearance is that the footlockers were found by a Japanese soldier, who, knowing nothing about fossils, simply dumped them out on the ground. And that, secretly, is what most authorities on the disappearance of the bones fear has happened. And yet, they are not sure—less sure now than ever.

After the war a variety of rumors about the Peking bones began to circulate. They had been seized by the Japanese and sent to the Emperor, who has a passionate interest in biology. In fact, the Emperor does have a passionate interest in biology, and several fossil finds were taken from territory conquered by the Japanese and sent back to Tokyo. The Japanese are known to have been on the lookout for the bones, but claim never to have found them. Given the confusion in China at that time, it is entirely possible that they did not. The Japanese government says that it knows nothing of the whereabouts of the bones, and there is no good reason to believe that it does.

The government of the People's Republic of China suspects that the bones may have been hidden and then spirited away to Taiwan with the retreating nationalists after the civil war. Or, alternately, that they really did reach America, where they are being kept from their rightful owners, the people of China, by American imperialists. Some Americans have countered that the Chinese Communists really possess the bones, but are keeping them out of sight for their own deviously Oriental reasons. None of these theories has much to recommend it.

More credible is the idea that somehow the fossils fell into the hands of a private party—Japanese, Chinese, American, or whatever—for several countries were involved in studying the bones in China. This individual has kept the treasure hidden, perhaps out of fear—for they had been stolen—or perhaps in hope of collecting a huge ransom at some later date. Try to imagine how you would feel if you knew that in your attic or cellar there was a treasure worth more than the Hope diamond —no, more than a dozen Hope diamonds—and that the governments of two of the most powerful nations on earth were looking for it. How would you act?

One of the private individuals who had become involved in the search was a Chicago businessman named Christopher Janus. Janus had offered a reward for information leading to the recovery of the fossils. One day he received a call from a woman who said that she had more than information, she had the fossils themselves.

The woman was both secretive and extremely nervous. She volunteered little over the telephone but suggested that they meet at the observatory atop the Empire State Building. Janus, while quite surprised by this melodramatic suggestion, agreed.

When he arrived at the Empire State Building observatory, he half-expected to find that he had been made the victim of a joke. But it was no joke. The woman, whom he describes as being a good-looking woman in her late forties, was there. She told him that her husband, who had since died, had come back from China after the war with a box full of fossils. At the time he warned her that it was very dangerous to possess these particular fossils, but that they were worth a lot of money. As proof, she showed Janus a picture of what appeared to be a box full of bones.

Then the woman noticed a group of tourists taking pictures. She panicked and rushed for the elevator, with Janus trailing behind her. "Didn't you see those people with a camera?" she said. "They were about to take a picture of me." Janus explained that the observatory of the Empire State Building was always filled with people taking pictures. The woman was not

114

convinced. She agreed only to call Janus back in a few days.

She did call, and demanded $500,000 for the fossils. She would not let experts examine them directly, but she did agree to let him have a copy of the photograph.

Unfortunately, the photograph settles nothing. Many experts have examined it, and most conclude that many of the bones shown are not those of Peking man. But a few of the bones, particularly a skull cap, are highly suggestive of the genuine article. They could, of course, be casts or models of the real skull—there is no way of telling from a photograph. But to the time of this writing the photograph is all that has become available. The searching and the hoping continue.

With the bones of Peking man and Livy's history of Rome, we are dealing with things that we know once existed, but have been lost. There is, however, another vast body of "lost secrets" which may or may not have existed. There is a tradition that in the past the ancients possessed knowledge of many things—but that much of this knowledge has been lost or hidden over the centuries. This belief is astonishingly persistent and powerful. It comes up in the most surprising ways. The idea seems to tie in with a general feeling that mankind once lived in a paradise —the Garden of Eden, The Golden Age, or what have you— but has fallen from that former high state. Along with the fall, so this tradition runs, mankind has lost a great deal of essential knowledge about the universe.

This idea has been the basis of a number of religions and secret societies which have claimed that they possessed a hidden body of knowledge. The information was revealed only to those initiates who had undergone rigorous testing and training. The tradition played a major role in the founding of groups like the

115

Masons. It is a bit hard to imagine that the Masonic lodges of today, which are essentially businessmen's social groups, were once regarded as the possessors of awesome and terrible secrets.

All of what we call "occultism" is really based on just such a tradition—for "occult" means "hidden." Representatives of practically every branch of occultism that you can name—from astrology to witchcraft—hint that they have access to a variety of "lost" or "hidden" secrets.

But there has probably been no activity in which this particular idea has been more important than in the practice of alchemy. Nearly everyone has heard of the alchemists who tried to turn base metals into gold. That was part of alchemy, but only part, for the alchemical quest was a broad one, aimed at uncovering all of what we would today call the secrets of nature.

The language of alchemy is confusing—often deliberately so. Creating the Philosopher's Stone was held to be the chief object of the alchemical experiment. But this "Stone" was most frequently described as a red or yellow powder that supposedly enabled the transmutation of base metal into gold. Yet another aim of the alchemist was the Elixir of Life that was supposed to confer eternal youth upon those who were fortunate enough to partake of it. Many alchemists appeared to regard the Elixir of Life as the soluble form of the Philosopher's Stone, though the language of the alchemists does not make this clear.

What concerns us in this inquiry, however, is the alchemist's belief that he was not discovering something new, but rather, rediscovering secrets or knowledge that had been lost or hidden. In addition to laboring over his furnaces and crucibles, the diligent alchemist also sought out old books and manuscripts, in

116

Nicolas Flamel

hope that the secret might be found in some forgotten work. He was also a persistent collector of tales and rumors—for there was always a rumor that someone somewhere had just rediscovered the Philosopher's Stone or the Elixir, but naturally was trying to keep it a secret.

One of the most instructive cases in the entire complex and tortured history of alchemy, is that of the fourteenth-century Parisian alchemist, Nicolas Flamel. Flamel was a scribe—that is, a document copyist—a substantial position in the days before printing. He had married a wealthy widow—to whom by all accounts he was utterly devoted—so he had more money and time at his disposal than most scribes.

As a scribe, Flamel naturally had an interest in books. One day a most curious volume fell into his hands. It was a very ancient book filled with strange drawings and inscriptions. According to an account of Flamel's discovery:

"Upon the first of the leaves there was written in large capital letters of gold: ABRAHAM THE JEW, PRINCE, LEVIT, ASTROLOGER

117

AND PHILOSOPHER TO THE NATION OF THE JEWS, BY THE WRATH
OF GOD DISPERSED AMONG THE GAULS SENDETH SALUTATION. After
this it was filled with great execrations and curses . . . against
every person that should cast his eyes upon it, unless he were
Sacrificer or Scribe."

Being a scribe, Flamel felt safe. Flamel knew that he had the
lost book of the Rabbi Abraham, which contained the formula
used by the Jews to make gold in order to pay the tribute due to
the Roman empire. The Jews were often credited and/or
blamed for possessing all sorts of secret knowledge.

The problem for Flamel was that the book appeared to be
written in a sort of code. He could understand part of it, but
not the key parts. This, by the way, is quite typical of alchemical writing. Flamel then set out on a search for some learned
Jew who might be able to help him unravel the puzzle of the
book. He finally found such a man, but even after the book was
translated, it still took Flamel years of experimenting to accom-
plish the "great work," that is, transmuting base metal into
gold. This was finally accomplished on the twenty-fifth of April,
1382. The only witness to the transformation was his faithful
wife, Pernelle.

Flamel was no King Midas, trying to turn everything into
gold. Indeed, he is said to have attempted the transmutation
only two more times in his life. He and his wife continued to
live in the same frugal and pious way as before. When he died
on March 22, 1417, he left behind a good reputation and a
modest fortune, which he willed to churches, hospitals, and
other charitable institutions.

But what of the book of Rabbi Abraham, and his formula for
making gold? It was never found, though Flamel's neighbors
thoroughly ransacked the alchemist's property after his death,
looking for it. The lure of Flamel's secrets remained strong, and

nearly two centuries after his death a local magistrate took possession of the property that had once belonged to the alchemist in order to thoroughly search it once again. But the searchers came up empty-handed.

The reasonable person can conclude that Flamel possessed no secret at all, and that he had either deluded himself, or had attempted to delude others. But alchemists were not a reasonable lot. The thought that they might someday discover Flamel's secret remained alive in their hearts for many hundreds of years.

Not only that, there was a rumor that, in addition to finding a way of transmuting base metals into gold, Flamel had also discovered the Elixir of Life, and that he and his wife had become immortal. Flamel's tombstone has been found; so has his wife's will. Yet they were both reportedly seen alive and well on several occasions long after they were supposed to have died.

At the beginning of the eighteenth century, Sieur Paul Lucas stated that during his travels in Asia Minor he had met a Moslem dervish, a student of alchemy and the Cabala (a book of Jewish mysticism), "who was a hundred years old although he seemed externally no more than thirty years." In addition, the dervish claimed to be a close friend of Flamel, though the French alchemist should have been dead for nearly three hundred years. Lucas reported the dervish as saying, "Neither he nor his wife have died; it is not above three years since I left them both in the Indies."

Another report held that the pair had been seen attending the opera in Paris in the mid-eighteenth century.

No one has seen Flamel recently, but another immortal alchemical adept named Fulcanelli is supposed to be operating in Europe at this very moment. We know that there was such a

119

person as Nicolas Flamel; we cannot be as sure of the existence of Fulcanelli. But the tale is an agreeably exotic one, and quite typical of the stories of mysterious personages and hidden secrets which swirl about in occult lore and give it much of its fascination.

There is a suspicion that the whole Fulcanelli tale was the invention of Julian Champagne, an occult painter with a strange sense of humor. The firsthand accounts of meetings with Fulcanelli are attributed to one Eugene Canseliet—who may or may not be another of Champagne's inventions. A letter attributed to Canseliet states that he met Fulcanelli in 1922, when the alchemist was already a very old man. "At the time he carried his eighty years lightly. Thirty years later I was to see him again and he then appeared to be a man of fifty."

Canseliet was then supposed to have become Fulcanelli's pupil, and learned how to transmute base metals into gold. But he learned other strange secrets as well. He was told that the Gothic cathedrals of Europe were much more than Christian monuments, that they served as repositories for a vast store of ancient knowledge. Fulcanelli held that all the secrets of alchemy—from the identification of the mysterious First Matter to the technique of transmutation—were expressed in the cathedrals, that "behind the gargoyles and the glyphs, the rose windows and the flying buttresses, a mighty secret lay, all but openly displayed . . . wholly unsuspected by the profane, the Gothic Cathedrals have for seven hundred years offered European man a course of instruction in his own possible evolution."

This idea that various structures, be they Gothic cathedrals or Egyptian pyramids, contain all sorts of secret knowledge actually built right into the structure is another familiar one in occult circles, and we will return to it again shortly.

The mysterious Canseliet is not the only one who has claimed to have encountered the even more mysterious Fulcanelli. Jacques Bergier, co-author of *Morning of the Magicians*, a book which became an international best-seller, said that he had met the immortal master in France during the Nazi occupation.

According to Bergier, the alchemist was thoroughly familiar with theoretical physics and atomic energy. Fulcanelli said that man had discovered nuclear energy in the forgotten past and that, as a result, the ancient civilizations had been so thoroughly destroyed that no trace of them could be found. Mankind had to struggle back from a state of primitive savagery into which it had been plunged by the destructive result of nuclear wars. Bergier reported Fulcanelli as saying that orthodox science was on the verge of discovering atomic fission (as indeed it was) and that unless suitable safeguards were created, mankind would once again blow itself back to barbarism.

There is not a shred of proof to support any of this. Indeed, even many devoted occultists regard such tales with great skepticism. But the mere fact that they continue to circulate in one form or another, as they have for centuries, indicates the appeal that such ideas have to a large number of people.

Bergier attributed to Fulcanelli the statement that there had been a great civilization in the distant past, which had been destroyed without a trace. But this idea has also been expressed by many others. It runs strongly through the legends surrounding Atlantis, which we discussed in Chapter 5. It also forms a basis for many of the "Gods from Outer Space" theories that have become so popular over the last few years.

Chariots of the Gods, the phenomenal best-seller by a Swiss writer named Erich von Däniken, contends that ancient astronauts brought civilization to earth some unknown thousands of years ago. As evidence of this, he points to old drawings and carvings which he contends show spaceships, and to legends which speak of gods coming out of the sky. He hints, much as Fulcanelli was supposed to have done, that the superior knowledge of the ancients was destroyed in a catastrophe, presumably a thermonuclear war, and is only today being rediscovered.

The idea that we were visited at some point in the distant past by intelligent beings from other planets, who brought civilization to us, is not original with von Däniken. This whole realm of theory is little more than an updating of the old lost Golden Age ideas which have been with us since the beginning of recorded history. Archaeologists and historians put no credence whatever in theories like those of von Däniken. They see them as wild and sensationalist speculations based on half-understood, and sometimes totally fraudulent, evidence. Yet the scorn of the professionals has not kept the theories from attaining wide popularity.

Without calling in superior beings from space, many, many others have found more than ample evidence of the lost secrets of the ancients. Traditionally, much of the speculation on the lost secrets has centered upon Egypt. This is because Egyptian civilization is very old (though not, as far as we can determine, the oldest). Its records are comparatively abundant, and the Egyptians were monumental builders. The pyramids were the first free-standing stone structures ever built, and they remained the largest man-made structures until modern times. They can still awe the traveler today. But were they built with secrets now lost?

Most archaeologists do not think so. Though there is a wide area of disagreement among scholars as to exactly how the pyramids and other Egyptian monuments were built, very few feel that it is necessary to call upon lost secrets to explain the construction methods. They credit the Egyptians' success in construction to painstaking use of simple tools and methods of calculation, and to the superb organization and discipline of a large work force over a long period of time.

But others gazing upon these marvelous structures have been gripped by the belief that "something else" had to be involved in the construction of the pyramids. This "something else" could have been a type of lever that modern science no longer knows about, or the secret of softening rocks with chemicals, or even the method for levitating huge blocks of stone and fitting them into their place in the monument. All of these ideas, and many hardly less bizarre, have seriously been proposed about the construction of the pyramids.

From here it is only a short step to proposing that not only were the pyramids built with the aid of techniques now lost, but that their very construction contains, in coded form, a huge variety of lost ancient knowledge. This is just what the elusive Fulcanelli said about Europe's Gothic cathedrals. The theories about the pyramids are, however, much older and more elaborate. They became so elaborate and widespread that the practice came to be called "pyramidology."

How did the pyramidologists infer that the ancient Egyptians had all sorts of "lost" knowledge hidden in the pyramids? They concentrated most of their attention on the Great Pyramid, largest and most celebrated of all Egypt's pyramids. The distance from the earth to the sun was only calculated in modern times. Yet according to the pyramidologists, the ancient Egyptians had also known this distance, and secreted the knowledge within the Great Pyramid, for if you take the height of the Great Pyramid (481 feet) and multiply it by one billion, the answer is approximately the distance from the earth to the sun

The Great Pyramid

in miles. Hard-working pyramidologists have found hundreds of correlations just like this one, in order to prove that the Egyptians knew an awful lot of things that they shouldn't have known.

Now it is easy to argue that, with so many numbers to play with, the pyramidologist can prove pretty nearly anything he wishes. Yet it is difficult to imagine just how strong a fascination these numerical correlations can hold for some people. Many highly intelligent people spent a good part of their lives and fortunes, as well as enduring ridicule and scorn, in the cause of pyramidology. Some of them even went beyond the concept that the pyramid contained all the wisdom of the past; they said that it also held the key to the future.

By manipulating measurements of the pyramids, they proved —to their own satisfaction at least—that the Great Pyramid had predicted all sorts of events that took place after it was built, and that it could still be used to predict the future. Pyramidologists were particularly good about predicting the end of the world. Different pyramidologists predicted different dates, and when those days passed without the world actually coming to an end, the practice of pyramidology began to look pretty foolish. It came to be regarded as nothing more than an eccentric historical curiosity. Even occultists tended to ignore it. But now, with growth of interest in lost secrets, pyramidology appears to be making something of a comeback.

Charles Piazzi Smyth, the Astronomer Royal of Scotland, was one of the foremost believers in the theory that all manner of ancient secrets were actually built into the structure of the Great Pyramid. His book, Our Inheritance in the Great Pyramid, *is the bible of pyramidology.*

The writer Peter Tompkins argued recently, in a highly popular book, that the Great Pyramid was more than a tomb for a dead king, but rather that it was an astronomical observatory, and that the Egyptians had an astronomical knowledge far beyond that with which conventional scholars credit them. Tompkins' argument was supported by the historian, Livio Catullo Stecchini, who says that he has proved that the Great Pyramid, and other Egyptian sites, were laid out according to a vast astronomical master plan.

An Orientalist named R. A. Schwaller de Lubicz proposed that in the building of the temple of Luxor, another huge Egyptian monument, could be found the key to certain cosmic laws. It was argued that these laws were not known by Egyptian society in general, but were the property of a secret society which operated out of that temple and a few others in Egypt. According to Schwaller, the dimensions of the temple were intended to express the laws pertaining to the function of growth. Thus, he said, the proportions of the temple are to the scale of an idealized human form. And the walls, chambers, colonnades, and sanctuaries that make up the temple reveal their cosmic function by their proportion, symbolic inscription, and position.

What are these "cosmic laws"? Schwaller's interpretation of the laws expressed at Luxor is extremely mathematical and complicated. Most scholars argue that these laws make no sense at all, and that Schwaller was merely indulging in the popular pastime of playing with numbers. The subject is too mathematical to ever attain great popularity, but still, Schwaller's ideas have made some converts—among them the British writer, John Anthony West. He has written:

"If the evidence presented by Schwaller is valid, ancient Egypt ceases to be merely an historical curio, but becomes an

126

According to one theory, the ancient Egyptian temple of Luxor is built to the scale of an idealized human form.

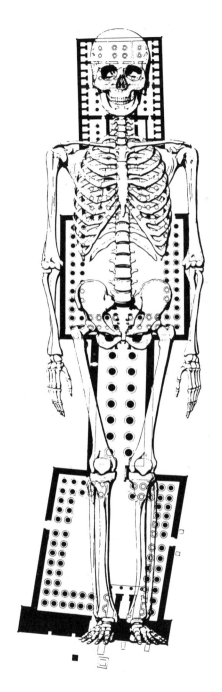

invaluable mine of scientific, medical, astronomical, astrological, mathematical, geological, magical, architectural, aesthetic and artistic knowledge. And this mine apparently stands ready to divulge its treasure, but only if it is approached in a proper frame of mind."

Egypt is not the only land in which the monuments have been subjected to this sort of unorthodox reinterpretation. For well

A great deal of controversy has always surrounded the question of who built the monument of Stonehenge and why.

over a century now, a huge variety of eccentric theories have been proposed about the monument, Stonehenge, in Britain. During the 1960s a distinguished astronomer said that the alignments of the stones in this monument showed that it had once been used as an astronomical observatory, and that the people who built it knew a great deal more about the movements of the heavens than previously believed. Most other scholars did not accept these theories—and still don't—but they are quite modest when compared to others that have been put forth over the years.

Some theories have held that not only Stonehenge, but many other ancient monuments, as well as churches, wayside crosses, sacred trees, and what have you, are all linked together in a vast network that outlines certain "natural lines of force" within the earth. These "natural lines of force" were known to the ancients, but the secret is lost to us.

More recently the monuments of the civilization of South America—the Incas and, most notably, the Mayas—have been subjected to the same sort of reappraisal by occultists and others who are convinced that the ancients, whoever they may be, knew an awful lot of things that we don't.

At the start of this chapter we told the story of a "lost" book which was supposed to have been found, at least briefly, in the palace of the Sultan in Turkey. We will close the chapter with another find of lost knowledge from the Imperial Palace in Constantinople. In 1929 a map was discovered in the palace that created a good deal of excitement. It was dated 1513 and signed with the name of Piri Re'is (Admiral Piri), an admiral of the Turkish navy.

The map showed that those who drew it were aware of the

129

existence of both North and South America—not really surprising, since it had been made over fifteen years after Columbus' discovery. But the map appeared to show the New World in more detail than other maps of the time. In addition, Piri Re'is stated in an inscription on the map that he had based his map on a map drawn by Columbus himself. This was an exciting statement, for there had long been rumors of a map drawn by Columbus, but that map had never been found. The Turks, who were going through a very nationalistic period just then, tried to make much of the Piri Re'is map, but few others were really interested in it, and the map sank back into obscurity.

It was rediscovered in the 1960s by Captain Arlington H. Mallery, a retired navigator who had spent years in the study of old maps. Mallery was not only interested in the Columbus statement, he was also interested in an inscription on the map which said that some of it had been based on maps dating back to the time of Alexander the Great. Even more interesting was the fact that the Piri Re'is map appeared to show the Antarctic continent, of which the sixteenth-century Turkish admiral could not possibly have known. But most intriguing of all, to Mallery's eyes, was that the map showed the Antarctic continent, not as it is today, when covered with ice, but as it must have appeared in times before the ice sheet covered it. The contours of the Antarctic continent under the ice were mapped in the late 1950s through the use of a variety of modern scientific techniques.

Mallery's suggestions were picked up by Professor Charles H. Hapgood, a man who has long championed highly unorthodox causes. With the aid of his students, Professor Hapgood examined the map, and other old maps, and came to the conclusion that medieval map-makers knew some things that we don't.

Professor Hapgood theorized that the map-makers were heirs to fragments of knowledge from a great civilization that had existed before the Ice Age, and which was somehow or another destroyed. He has written:

"The evidence presented by the ancient maps appears to suggest the existence in remote times, before the rise of any of the known cultures, of a true civilization, of a comparatively advanced sort, which either was localized in one area but had worldwide commerce, or was, in a real sense a *worldwide* culture. The culture, at least in some respects, may well have been more advanced than the civilizations of Egypt, Babylonia, Greece and Rome."

Such a theory has not attracted any large number of supporters from among the ranks of professional archaeologists or historians. Indeed, most, if they have heard of it at all, would regard such an idea as absurd. What of Antarctica on the Piri Re'is map? That, say the critics, is merely a conventional representation of the Great Southern Continent, which most cartographers assumed, for all the wrong reasons, had to exist. The relationship between the outline sketched on the Piri Re'is map, and the continental mass beneath the Antarctic ice, is not terribly striking. It can be made to "fit," say the critics, only through a generous application of wishful thinking.

But such criticism does not go to the heart of the matter of interest in such things as the Piri Re'is map. It isn't the particular piece of evidence that really matters. What matters is the pervasive feeling that there is much knowledge and many secrets that were known a long time ago, but have over the centuries been lost or hidden.

131

8

Mysterious Appearances

If things—people, ships, planes, and the like—disappear mysteriously, can the process be reversed? Can things appear mysteriously as well? The answer seems to be yes. There are not nearly as many mysterious appearances in history as mysterious disappearances—or at least the subject has never attracted as much attention—but still there are notable cases.

Unquestionably, the best known of these is the case of Kaspar Hauser. Hauser came wandering apparently out of nowhere and into the streets of Nuremberg in Bavaria on May 26, 1828.

He was a strongly built lad in his mid-teens. He was wearing poorly fitting clothes, he limped badly, and was carrying a letter addressed to "The Captain of the 4th Squadron, 6th Cavalry Regiment, in Nuremberg." The boy was directed to the military post, where he was then told to wait until the captain returned. He startled those around him by trying to pick up a candle by the flame, and burning his hand in the process. He gave every indication of being entirely unacquainted with fire.

He also had a very limited vocabulary; he answered practically every question with the words *"Weiss nicht"* ("Don't know"). Most of the time he just mumbled incoherently.

When the captain arrived, he opened the envelope that was addressed to him. It contained two letters. The first read:

Honored Captain,

I send you a lad who wishes to serve his king in the Army. He was brought to me on October 7th, 1812. I am but a poor laborer with children of my own to rear. His Mother asked me to bring up the boy, and so I thought I would rear him as my own son. Since then I have never let him go one step outside the house, so no one knows where he was reared. He, himself, does not know the name of the place or where it is.

You may question him, Honored Captain, but he will not be able to tell you where I live. I brought him out at night. He cannot find his way back. He has not a penny, for I have nothing myself. If you will not keep him, you must strike him dead or hang him.

The message was neither dated nor signed. The other note was dated October, 1812. It read:

This child has been baptized. His name is Kaspar; you must give him his second name yourself. I ask you to take care of him. His father was a cavalry soldier. When he is seventeen, take him to Nuremberg, to the Sixth Cavalry Regiment; his father belonged to it. I beg you to keep him until he is seventeen. He was born on April 30th 1812. I am a poor girl; I can't take care of him. His father is dead.

The outline of the story indicated by the two notes was plausible enough. A baby, probably the illegitimate son of a

133

Engraving showing Kaspar Hauser as he looked when he first appeared in Nuremberg in May, 1828.

soldier, is born to a poor girl. She leaves the infant on the door-step of a family, perhaps farmers, with a note asking them to take care of him and raise him to be a soldier. Out of a sense of responsibility the family keeps the child, but out of a sense of shame he is hidden from neighbors. When he is old enough the boy is turned out on the world, in the hopes that he will make his way as a soldier.

There was, however, one problem with the story—both of the notes were fakes. It did not take long to discover that both had been written by the same person, though there had been a clumsy attempt to disguise the handwriting. Moreover, both notes were quite recent.

Besides the notes the boy had no clue to his identity. His pockets contained only a rosary, a few printed religious tracts, and a packet of salt. The boy himself was most unhelpful in establishing his own identity. He was given a pencil and piece of paper and asked to write his name and address. He scrawled the words Kaspar Hauser, but nothing else. To questions about his past he replied, "Don't know."

The strange boy was examined, and found to be about seven-teen years old, and in good health. Observers first thought that Kaspar was crippled, because he limped so badly when he walked. The examination showed that the only thing wrong with him was that his feet were badly blistered, perhaps because his boots did not fit him, or he was unused to walking.

Not knowing what else to do with him, the captain turned him over to the police. The police locked Kaspar in a cell "for observation." He didn't seem to mind. He could sit rigidly for hours, with no apparent sign of boredom or discomfort. The simplest things like a watch or a coin seemed to provide him with endless amusement.

At first it was assumed that the boy was feebleminded. This would have explained a great deal. It was an era in which the mentally retarded were often hidden from view. A feebleminded child who had grown too old and troublesome to be hidden any longer might have been turned out by his parents, and given false letters in order to disguise the place of his origin.

But Kaspar Hauser was not feebleminded, as the authorities quickly discovered. In addition to his name, and "don't know," the boy appeared to know just a few other words. One of them was "horse," a word he seemed to apply to all animals, another was "soldier," and another was "boy," a word he used for both sexes.

Then, with astonishing speed, the boy appeared to acquire a very fluent vocabulary. In addition, he learned to read and write, and handle various utensils like knives and lanterns, of which he had originally seemed totally unfamiliar.

Within two months he had picked up enough of a vocabulary to tell his own story, and a very odd story it was too. For as long as he could remember, said Kaspar Hauser, he had lived in a tiny dark cell, in which there was not even enough room to stand up or walk.

Often when he woke up, he found a jug of water and a loaf of dark bread waiting for him. When he first appeared, Kaspar Hauser would only eat bread and water; other food made him sick. He said that occasionally the water would have a strange bitter taste, and after drinking it he would fall into an unusually deep sleep. When he awoke he found that his clothes, and the straw that served as his bed, had been changed and his nails and hair were cut. The only other objects in Kaspar Hauser's cell were three wooden horses.

Kaspar Hauser said that he had no idea how long this strange existence continued; not ever having known any other, he accepted it without being bored or unhappy.

Then one day his whole life changed. A man entered his cell. He taught the boy how to write the name, KASPAR HAUSER, and how to speak the few words like "horse" and "don't know," which appeared to have made up his entire original vocabulary. Somewhat later Kaspar drank some of the bitter water and fell into one of his deep sleeps. When he awoke he was wearing new clothes and boots, for the first time in his life. He was led out of the cell into the open air. His memory of the journey, he said, remained foggy, though he could recall that his feet hurt as he walked. He had no idea where he had come from, how far he had walked. Nor could he describe in any detail what the man who had brought him out looked like.

The story was a sensational one, and it made Kaspar a celebrity, not only in Nuremberg, but throughout Germany. But the story, like the letters, was also quite obviously false. If the boy had been kept in a lightless cell all his life, or even for a few months, he would have been noticeably pallid, yet Kaspar Hauser's color was quite normal. If he had been preventing from standing up or walking about for sixteen years, he probably would have been unable to walk at all. He certainly would have shown more dramatic signs of his confinement than blistered feet after his first walk to Nuremberg.

Despite this very obvious discrepancy in his story, most people seemed to take it pretty much at face value. They assumed that Kaspar had been the illegitimate son of some important person, for who but an important person would be willing or able to go to such lengths to hide the boy? The great guessing game was, which important person? Practically everybody with any degree of standing at all was implicated by rumor.

Because of his new fame, Kaspar was taken from his cell—where he had been more or less on public display—and lodged in the house of Professor Georg Friedrich Daumer, a local lecturer with an interest in "magnetism"—that is, hypnotism, a subject which enjoyed a tremendous vogue among the well-educated folk of Germany at that time. For a while Kaspar Hauser became the guest at parties of the best families in Nuremberg. Every once in a while he would come up with some new tidbit of information about his past. None of it, however, was very enlightening, nor did it help to discover where he had come from and who he was.

After a while, though, the novelty of the mystery boy began to wear off and interest in him declined. Then something happened which once again catapulted Kaspar Hauser to public attention. On the afternoon of October 7, 1829, Kaspar was found unconscious on the floor of Professor Daumer's cellar. He had a nasty looking gash on his forehead and his shirt was torn. The wound turned out not to be serious. The boy said that he had been attacked by a man wearing dark clothes, leather gloves, and a silken mask. Kaspar said he had been attacked with either a knife or a club—the accounts differ and it is possible that the boy gave different stories, or genuinely did not know.

There was an immediate search launched for the masked assailant, and though many people claimed to have seen the masked man, the stories were so inconsistent that the police assumed, probably correctly, that they were either mistakes or outright fabrications.

A lot of people thought that the highly placed person who had fathered Kaspar, and then hidden him, had now sent a

One of the last pictures made of Kaspar Hauser during his lifetime. He had become quite a dandy.

hired killer to get rid of the boy, once and for all. But there were also skeptics. They had doubted Kaspar's tales from the first, and now they claimed that the attack was a fraud. The wound was superficial and could easily have been self-inflicted. Why would a potential assassin render his victim unconscious, and then just cut him on the head? The skeptics said that Kaspar had staged the attack and made up the story, to attract attention when his fame appeared to be slipping.

Kaspar did manage to attract the attention of one very important person—Lord Stanhope, wealthy member of a prominent English family. Lord Stanhope paid a special visit to Nuremberg in order to meet the boy, and was impressed. He returned several other times, and seemed to strike up a genuine friendship with Kaspar.

Kaspar left Professor Daumer's house under circumstances that are not really clear. He then went to a number of different residences in the city. But more and more people in Nuremberg began to complain that the boy was a fraud, living off the generosity and stupidity of the people of the city. So, when Lord Stanhope offered to take over supervision of the boy, Nuremberg authorities jumped at the opportunity to get him off their hands. Kaspar Hauser, they felt, had become a lot more trouble than he was worth. German aristocrats, whom rumor had saddled with Kaspar's paternity, were threatening legal action, and it was reported that a duel was fought over the matter and several more were in the offing.

Kaspar was placed under the protection of an old lawyer named Paul Johann von Feuerbach, who was in the process of compiling a report on the boy and is the primary source of information on the case. But Feuerbach died before his report was published, leading to another round of rumors. At this time Lord Stanhope suggested that Kaspar Hauser be taken to quieter surroundings. The place chosen was the nearby village of Ansbach, where he was placed under the care of a teacher named Meyer. A local military officer, Captain Hickel, was given the responsibility for his security.

For a short time Kaspar Hauser was the center of a social whirl in Ansbach. But it was a small place, and the novelty of the boy from nowhere soon wore off, and he sank into obscurity once again.

140

Then, on December 14, 1833, there was to be one final spectacular moment in the strange Kaspar Hauser saga. It was a snowy Saturday afternoon and Kaspar Hauser had gone out walking in the park. He returned to Meyer's house clutching his right side. Blood was dripping through his coat. Meyer asked him what had happened and he gasped, "Man stabbed!—Knife!—Hofgarten!—Gave purse!—Go look quickly!"

As Kaspar was undressed it was obvious that he had a knife wound in his right side below the rib cage. But it did not appear to be a serious wound and there was no immediate concern for his life.

Captain Hickel went to the Hofgarten, which was the town's public park, as Kaspar had asked. There was no sign of an assailant with a knife, but Hickel did find a silk purse, and the purse did contain a note.

The characters of the note were unintelligible at first, and could be read only after being held up to a mirror. Even after the note was read it didn't make much sense.

"Hauser will be able to tell you how I look, whence I came from, and who I am. To spare him that task, I will tell you myself. I am from . . . On the Bavarian border . . . On the river . . . My name is 'M.L.O.' "

The trouble was that Hauser couldn't, or wouldn't, tell very much. He said that earlier he had been given a note telling him to meet a man in the park. Kaspar described the man as "tall, with dark whiskers, wearing a black cloak." The man handed Kaspar a purse and then stabbed him, and fled.

A wide search was organized for the black-cloaked stranger, but no one was found fitting the description. More intriguingly, however, when the area where Kaspar had been stabbed was examined, Captain Hickel noticed something very peculiar about it. There was only one set of footprints in the snow; they were Kaspar's. If he had met anyone the stranger was floating off the ground.

Kaspar was severely taxed with these questions. But he continued to insist that he had met a stranger who had stabbed him. What's more, his condition took an alarming turn for the worse. On the afternoon of December 17 Kaspar Hauser went into a coma, and that evening he died. Tradition has it that his final words were, "I didn't do it myself."

A post-mortem showed that a knife or some other sharp instrument had cut through his diaphragm and penetrated the point of the heart. Of the three physicians who examined the body, one said that the wound could not have been self-inflicted, two others were not sure. Kaspar Hauser's posthumous fame surpassed any that he had attained during the five and a half years of his strange public existence.

After Kaspar's death Feuerbach's long delayed volume was published. The old jurist had accepted Kaspar's stories entirely and concluded that the boy must have been in line for a very powerful position, for otherwise no one would have bothered with such elaborate confinement. He was released, Feuerbach reasoned, only after someone else had taken the place for which he was destined. However, when Kaspar's appearance created so much furor, the powerful persons who had hidden him tried to do away with him.

Though Feuerbach did not say who the guilty parties might be, it was obvious to everyone that he had in mind the Grand Dukes of Baden. In that family all the heirs of the regular line had died in fairly rapid succession. There was a rumor that they had been killed, in order to make room for the son of the reigning duke's young mistress.

142

Feuerbach's theory had no basis outside of Kaspar's own incredible tales, but the ruling family of Baden soon gave it one by having the book banned in their lands, and prevailing upon friendly rulers to ban it in their territories. This act of aristocratic stupidity made Feuerbach's book more popular than ever.

Kaspar Hauser became sort of a folk hero. There is a memorial erected at the place where he was stabbed. Its inscription reads: "On this place for mysterious reasons one mysterious figure was murdered by another mysterious figure."

His gravestone has a similarly tantalizing inscription: "Here lies Kaspar Hauser, Riddle of Our Time. His Birth was Unknown; his Death Mysterious."

There is a small Kaspar Hauser museum in Nuremberg which houses a collection of memorabilia of the case. An enormous amount has been written about it—and yet in the century and a half since Kaspar Hauser's death, no new material evidence has been turned up.

The best guess is that Kaspar Hauser was a psychopath, who thrived on attention and had made up the story about his imprisonment, and had also twice wounded himself to attract attention. The second time he had not meant to stab himself so deeply. Yet who was he, really, and where did he come from? We still don't know.

Aside from assigning Kaspar Hauser to most of the crowned heads of Europe, and the bulk of the Catholic Church hierarchy, authors have had even wilder suggestions. Charles Fort speculated—though it is impossible to tell how serious he was— that Kaspar was a representative of a mysterious civilization that existed beneath the North Pole. Fort went on to wonder if Kaspar was not murdered because he was about to reveal what

Cagliostro

he knew about this civilization. Other writers have suggested that Kaspar Hauser came from another planet or another dimension.

While Kaspar Hauser remains the best known of those figures who some believe appeared mysteriously upon the earth, he is certainly not the only one. Fort was also fascinated by Cagliostro, a late eighteenth-century alchemist and occultist. Fort seemed to believe that Cagliostro appeared from nowhere, possessing near superhuman knowledge.

On the other hand, there is considerable hard evidence to suggest that Cagliostro was, in fact, one Joseph Balsamo, a Sicilian swindler. If Cagliostro had possessed superhuman knowledge, then it was not sufficient to keep him from coming to a very bad end. He died miserably, a prisoner in a rock-cut dungeon in the Castel Sant' Angelo near the Vatican. Yet there are those who claimed that Cagliostro didn't die at all, but escaped from the inescapable fortress, and lives still!

A better candidate for mysterious appearances is Cagliostro's older contemporary and apparent idol, the Count de Saint-Germain. Saint-Germain was a genuinely mysterious character, who moved with ease and familiarity through circles of the rich and powerful of Europe. He was rumored to possess all manner of alchemical secrets, including the Elixir of Life. Some people said that they had first met Saint-Germain some fifty or sixty years before, and he had not aged a day in all that time. The Count is reported to have told stories of how he was a companion of many historical figures, like Richard the Lion-Hearted whom he had accompanied on the crusades.

But the Count never really made any claims at all. He was a charming, well-educated fellow, with an excellent memory and a good knowledge of history. Unlike many of his contemporaries, he did not indulge himself in overeating or overdrinking and thus managed to remain youthful looking. Moderation, he often said, was the true Elixir of Life. As for the rest, he said very little—he simply did not contradict other people when they said outrageous things about him.

Who was he, really? Where did he come from? Those questions remain as much of a mystery today as they were in Saint-Germain's own time. He was certainly no count, but most probably a man of humble origins and lively intelligence, who had discovered a pretty good way of getting through life. He is reputed to have died at the court of a princely admirer in about 1782, though there are those who claim to have run into him much more recently.

The mysterious stranger who buys a big and isolated house, leaving all the townsfolk to wonder and guess as to his origins, is

145

almost a stock character in fiction. Yet history provides a few authentic examples of this type.

One of the best known of these cases concerns the couple that arrived suddenly and unexpectedly in the town of Ingelfingen, in what is now East Germany, in the year 1803. Not much ever happened at Ingelfingen, so the arrival of any strangers at all was bound to be noticed, and one could hardly help but notice this couple.

They arrived by carriage. Both were elegantly dressed. The woman's face was entirely hidden from view by a thick veil, though from the lightness of her step, the townsfolk assumed that she was quite young. The couple rented a suite of rooms, and hired a local woman to do the domestic work. Otherwise they were attended only by a coachman-valet, who seemed very nearly as mysterious as his master and mistress.

The mysterious gentleman did occasionally go about the town and speak to people, but he never gave his name. People began calling him the Count, a title he neither affirmed nor denied. The lady was more withdrawn. She would leave her apartment only to take a drive in the countryside, or to take a walk in the secluded garden of the house, and always she was heavily veiled.

At the time Europe was full of French aristocrats fleeing the revolutionary government in their homeland. Most people simply assumed that the strangers were just such *émigrés*. One morning, as the lady was riding in her carriage, a gust of wind blew her veil aside for a moment. Those who saw her face in that brief time said that she bore a striking resemblance to the daughter of Louis XVI, the King of France, beheaded by the revolutionaries.

The woman who was employed by the pair could add little to the story. She had never seen the lady's face, though she also affirmed that from her movements the woman appeared to be quite young. She also knew that the Count received a large number of letters from foreign countries. She gave the gossips precious little to work with.

One day, a few months after the pair arrived at Ingelfingen, they were gone. They had taken their leave, early in the morning, before most of the townsfolk were awake.

People gossiped for a while, and then the story was forgotten. Six years later, however, the people of Ingelfingen were once again reminded of the pair when they heard that the same couple, or their exact counterparts, had taken up residence in the neighboring town of Hildburghausen, where they were behaving in the same mysterious manner.

This time the man had picked up a name; he was called Count Vavel de Versay, though whether the man had actually claimed the title, or merely allowed others to claim it for him without contradicting them is unclear. After a few months of lodging in a rented suite of rooms, the couple moved, but not very far. They purchased an old chateau on the outskirts of the town of Eishausen, about nine miles from Hildburghausen.

Inevitably a variety of stories circulated about the couple at Eishausen. Considerable controversy developed among the townsfolk as to the lady's age. It had been over six years since she was first reported as being quite young—when she had come to Ingelfingen. Yet many said that she was still quite young. But one man, a road mender, who happened to see the lady's carriage pass regularly, insisted that there were really two ladies, one young and beautiful and the other old and ugly. And that they took turns going out in the carriage.

A young gardener at the chateau (one of the few servants the Count hired) claimed that the lady was beautiful and had once smiled at him and spoken to him. At that moment, said the

The daughter of the executed king of France, Louis XVI, who was believed by many to be the "mystery lady" of Eishausen.

gardener, the Count appeared, dragged the lady off by the arm, and threatened him. The story may have been true, but it sounds more like a young man's boast.

It was at about this time that Kaspar Hauser reached the pinnacle of his fame. Some people decided that the mysterious boy must in some way be connected with the mysterious couple. It was reported that Kaspar was actually brought to the estate at Eishausen and shown its exterior. Those who brought him fully expected that he would identify the estate as the place he had been kept before coming to Nuremberg. But Kaspar professed complete ignorance of the place, and the attempt to connect these two popular mysteries failed.

Then one day, some five years after the couple had moved to

the chateau at Eishausen, the Count announced that the lady had died, and was to be buried in the garden of another house that he owned in Hildburghausen. The funeral was quite public. When the officiating clergyman asked for the name and date of birth of the Count's "wife," he replied that the dead woman was not his wife, and that he could say nothing of her. Later, however, it was reported that the woman was buried under the name, Sophie Botta, and that she was a spinster, a native of Westphalia, and fifty-eight years of age.

The coffin was open during the services, and it was rumored that many of those who looked into it saw not a corpse, but a large wax doll. There were also rumors that a short time after the funeral a coach driven by four very powerful horses left the chateau. The coach was being driven at a furious pace, and all the blinds were tightly drawn. Who or what was in the coach? Residents disagreed, but it did provide them with a lot to talk about.

The local authorities could find nothing irregular about the lady's death and burial, and since the Count contributed generously to local charities, the authorities were not disposed to press the matter too closely.

The Count lived on at Eishausen for many years, finally dying there in 1845. When his estate was examined, it was discovered that he had considerably less money than most people had thought. The big surprise was a baptismal register and other papers indicating that the Count was, in fact, Leonard Cornelius Van der Valck, originally from Amsterdam.

Eventually some Van der Valck relatives arrived from Amsterdam to claim what there was of the mystery man's property. The authorities accepted the claim. But the people of the vicinity of Eishausen did not. And lovers of the strange and mysterious from that day to this have never been comfortable with the identification of the mysterious Count Vavel de Versay with the simple Cornelius Van der Valck.

Letters addressed to Cornelius an der Valck had been delivered to the chateau during the "Count's" lifetime, though no one seems to have connected them with the Count. Not one of the living Van der Valck relatives had ever seen the man in person, so they could not testify from firsthand knowledge that he really was Van der Valck. Elliott O'Donnell, a collector of strange stories, sums up his doubts this way:

"Besides, it must be admitted that if the Count were no Count at all, but a man of distinctly middle-class origin, such as a man of the name of Van der Valck would be, his assumption of aristocracy 'sat on him' exceedingly well, since no one ever doubted his veracity when he alluded to certain members of the Bourbon family as people whom he had known intimately, nor did they even dream that he might be drawing the long bow, when he talked of having been to Vienna for the express purpose of meeting the Emperor Alexander. Hence, his appearance and manners, which were undoubtedly those of an extremely cultured and aristocratic man, negates the theory that he was Cornelius Van der Valck. But, if he were not Cornelius Van der Valck, who was he?"

O'Donnell was something of the snob in his easy assumption that a commoner with the humble name of Van der Valck would be unable to impersonate successfully a count, or a king, for that matter. But still, it is a point. If this man had spent years saying, or allowing others to say, that he was a count, is it not also possible that the Van der Valck identification was an impersonation as well?

Nor does the Van der Valck identification answer all the

other questions raised by this case. What about the apparent eternal youth of the lady, or the problem of the two ladies? Was someone named Sophie Botta really in the coffin that was buried in the garden, or was it a wax doll as others claimed? Perhaps the entire "mystery" is the result of rumor and gossip that accumulated around a pair that, for entirely personal reasons, did not wish to mix with their neighbors. At this late date there is no way of really knowing.

And there are other mysterious folk—many, many others. There was the man in the monk's robe, who was described as having the face of a healthy corpse, and who called himself Father Cyprian of the Society of Jesus. In fact, there was no Father Cyprian of the Society of Jesus. But before this was discovered, the fellow had become involved in an incident which also involved the Marquise de Maintenon, first mistress and then wife of Louis XI, and ended in the murder of a young nobleman. The identity of the bogus Father Cyprian was never discovered, nor was he ever seen again.

In 1947 a man calling himself the Maha Chochan or Kut Hami appeared in Paris. He said that he was the leader of the Great Universal White Brotherhood that lived in a fabulous underground city called the Agartha. A place called the Agartha figures prominently in some occult lore, and so does the Great Universal White Brotherhood, though there is not a scrap of evidence that either really exists.

The Maha Chochan even gave a press conference. One of the questions was "concerning the legend that Saint John was still alive and waiting in Tibet for the return of Christ."

Nonsense, replied the Maha Chochan. Everyone in the Agar-

151

tha knew for a fact that St. John had died, in the twelfth century, in Tibet.

To prove his authenticity the Maha Chochan said that he was going to perform a genuine miracle. Unfortunately, he disappeared from the scene before the miracle could be performed.

I myself have met several people who claim, in all seriousness, that they were born on Saturn or some other planet, and were teleported to earth or dropped off by a UFO. You may feel that we have strayed from the genuinely mysterious to the obviously foolish. Yet in this day of walks on the moon there is nothing inherently more foolish about a story of coming from another planet than there was in Kaspar Hauser's story of being kept in a tiny cell. There were plenty who thought Kaspar Hauser was a fraud, or mad, but he had his supporters. So do the people who say they come from other planets, though none of them has ever attained the fame of a Kaspar Hauser, and in most cases their backgrounds are well known, and quite ordinary.

In any event, the idea that people can appear from nowhere, or at least from some place very strange, is still around, as is the idea that people and things can disappear into nowhere, or at least into some place very strange. In our final chapter we are going to try and tie some of these beliefs together and see what they mean—or what they don't mean.

9

What's Going On Here?

From Judge Crater to Kaspar Hauser, we have told some pretty strange stories. Is there a mysterious "something" which ties all, or many, of these tales together? In recent years a lot of people have come to think so. Witness the tremendous popularity of the Bermuda Triangle idea.

Charles Fort had speculated on the possibility that Kaspar Hauser was the representative of an unknown civilization from beneath the North Pole. He also toyed with the idea that people or ships or planes had been kidnapped by spaceships from other planets. Fort had never heard the terms flying saucer or UFO—these became popular in the 1940s and Charles Fort died in 1932—but he had certainly collected a large number of accounts of what we might call UFOs. He also speculated rather more extensively on the idea of teleportation—that is, the instantaneous transfer of matter from one place to another.

"The look to me," Fort wrote, "is that, throughout what is loosely called Nature, teleportation exists, as a means of distribution of things and materials, and that sometimes human

153

beings have command, mostly unconsciously, though perhaps sometimes as a development from research and experiments, of this force." Fort seemed to believe that teleportation was one of those lost secrets that we were discussing.

Those who, like Charles Fort, suspected that there was a great deal in heaven and earth not dreamed of in scientific philosophy continued to speculate upon the mysterious disappearances and discuss such ideas as extraterrestrial kidnappings and teleportation. Then, in the mid-1950s, all of the speculations and rumors seemed to come together in the extraordinary affair that came to be known as the Philadelphia Experiment.

In the tight little world inhabited by those of us interested in strange mysteries and weird theories a rumor began to circulate. The substance of the rumor was that during World War II around the year 1943 the U.S. Navy, in a classified experiment to test invisibility, had accidentally teleported a warship with all its crew from its berth in Philadelphia to Newport, Virginia. The ship appeared in Newport only for an instant, the rumor ran, and then reappeared in Philadelphia. The Navy, however, abandoned invisibility experiments when it was discovered that many of the sailors aboard the ship had been driven insane or worse by the experience.

The story is, quite obviously, a sensational one. Had the U.S. Navy accidentally discovered the lost secret of teleportation? Had the Navy even been experimenting with invisibility? The information was supposed to have been top secret, so when the Navy denied knowing anything about such a project, this did not seem surprising.

But how had the rumor gotten started in the first place? As far as anyone has been able to determine, it began with a man named Morris K. Jessup. Jessup had worked professionally in

Charles Fort

the field of radio astronomy, and he had also become fascinated by the subject of Unidentified Flying Objects. In 1955 he wrote a book called *The Case for the UFO*.

On January 13, 1956, Jessup said that he received a strange letter from a man named Carlos Miguel Allende, who also used the Americanized version of his name, Carl M. Allen. The letter had been mailed from Texas but gave a Pennsylvania return address.

The letter, which was quite long and rambling, gave an account of the strange "Philadelphia Experiment." It mentioned Einstein and the Unified Field theory, and indicated that Einstein's work was completed by "my friend Dr. Franklin Reno." The document was poorly spelled, and written in a very curious prose style. This passage from it will give you an idea:

"The 'result' [of the experiment] was complete invisibility of a ship, destroyer type, and all its crew, while at sea (Oct. 1943). The field was effective in an oblate spheroidal shape, extending one hundred yards (more or less) out from each beam of the ship. Any person within that sphere became vague in form, but he too observed those persons aboard the ship as though they too were of the same state, yet were walking upon nothing. Any person without that sphere could see nothing save the clearly defined shape of the ship's hull in the water, providing of course, that that person was just close enough to see, yet just barely outside of the field."

The writer implied that he had witnessed the reappearance of the ship in Norfolk in October, 1943, from the deck of a Matson Lines liberty ship out of Norfolk.

According to the letter: "Half of the officers and crew of that ship are at present mad as hatters. A few are, even yet, confined to certain areas where they may receive trained scientific aid when they either 'go blank and get stuck' . . . or else when he 'freezes.'" Going blank meant becoming temporarily invisible; freezing meant that a man could not move of his own volition.

Allende reported that only a few of the afflicted crewmen had survived. "One just walked through his quarter's wall in sight of his wife and child and two other crew members (was never seen again), and two 'went into the flame', i.e. they 'froze' and caught fire while carrying common small-boat compasses. One man carried the compass and caught fire, the other came for the 'laying on of hands' as he was nearest, but he too took fire."

Somewhat farther on in the letter Allende wrote, "I wish to mention, that somehow, also, the experimental ship disappeared from its Philadelphia dock and only a very few minutes later appeared at its other dock in the Norfolk, Newport News, Portsmouth area. This was distinctly and clearly identified as being that place, but the ship again disappeared and went back to its Philadelphia dock in only a very few minutes or less. This was also noted in the newspapers, but I forget what paper I read it in or when it happened. Probably late in the experiments, may have been in 1956 after experiments were discontinued, I cannot say for sure."

Obviously the Allende letter was a very, very strange one, full of difficult-to-follow phrases, and outright contradictions—for example, where the writer in one place implies that he had witnessed the appearance of the ship at Norfolk, and in another place he indicates that he read about it in the newspapers.

Just how seriously Morris K. Jessup took this peculiar correspondence is rather difficult to say, but he did send a postcard to the Pennsylvania address and about four months later received a second letter from the mysterious Carlos Allende.

This second letter added only a few details, but contained Allende's offer to be questioned while hypnotized, or under the influence of a "truth serum." He also said that any of those involved in the incident who were still alive would benefit from being hypnotized, for no one could really recall all of the details of what had happened without the aid of hypnosis. The letter ended with:

"Perhaps already the Navy has used this accident of transport to build your UFO's. It is a logical advance from any stand-point. What do you think?"

Between the two letters, Jessup received another interesting document. It was a paperback copy of his own book, with several hundred comments scribbled in the margins in different colored inks. Among the comments hinting at intimate knowledge of UFOs, where they came from and what they were doing, Jessup found some veiled references to a secret Navy experiment and an invisible ship. He also felt that some of the comments were written in the same style as the Allende letter, and he became convinced that Allende added notations to the book, although he may have been only one of several persons to have done so.

The book had originally been mailed to the Office of Naval Research from Texas. It drifted down through channels and was finally given to Jessup one day when he visited the office in Washington. He was quite sure that the Navy believed that the annotations had great significance.

A tragic twist in this curious tale came on the evening of April 20, 1959, when the body of Morris K. Jessup was found in his station wagon in Dade County Park, near Coral Gables, Florida. A hose ran from the car's exhaust pipe to the inside of the closed car.

Vincent Gaddis, the man who first coined the phrase, "the Bermuda Triangle," notes ominously, "The death certificate lists the cause as suicide."

A belief or suspicion that there was something irregular or mysterious about Jessup's death, and that it was somehow or another connected with the Allende letters, and that it was all somehow tied up with a great mystery, or great conspiracy or both, circulated for years among UFO buffs and others of a similar inclination. A couple of books were written about the subject, though they received only a limited circulation, limited primarily to the hard core of UFO buffs. They also added nothing of value to the story.

Still, a lot of people had heard something about the Philadelphia Experiment, or the Allende letters, or of the "scientist" who had been mysteriously "killed" because he knew too much about the experiment. Vincent Gaddis devoted an entire chapter of his book on mysteries of the sea, *Invisible Horizons*, to the Philadelphia Experiment. Charles Berlitz, whose book, *The Bermuda Triangle*, was the most widely read on the subject, also discussed the Philadelphia Experiment at length. So the story has been spread far beyond the circle of UFO and strange-mystery buffs. The impression has gotten around that the Philadelphia Experiment is not only connected with the Bermuda Triangle, but with all sorts of mysterious disappearances.

What's the truth? Let's first clear up Jessup's death. There is absolutely no reason to believe that Jessup's death was anything other than a suicide. Paris Flammonde, who once produced an all-night radio talk show on which Jessup had frequently appeared, has written this about him:

"Jessup, who had some severe personal problems, contacted Long John Nebel [host of the radio program] just before his death, suggesting that he was seriously considering suicide. He requested that, should such a tragic course be pursued by him, a séance be conducted on Mr. Nebel's all-night radio program. The purpose of this plan was to give John, who had assisted him in a number of ways, the incredible story, should such a return prove possible. The program, completely arranged and about to go on the air, was aborted by Mr. Nebel's attorney, who felt that the privacy of certain persons might be violated."

So Morris K. Jessup, the man about whom the whole tale of

the Philadelphia Experiment appears to center, was a deeply troubled man.

What of the elusive Carlos Allende? No authentic trace of him has ever been found. The Allende letter, and the annotated copy of Jessup's book, may seem startling and inexplicable to many people. But anyone who has written articles and books on strange subjects is likely to get an awful lot of strange mail— often couched in the same sort of twisted prose as the Allende letters, or written in margins in varicolored inks, as were the annotations on the Jessup book.

I have, over the years, collected a whole boxful of similar material. In the early 1960s I received a series of letters from a fellow who asserted, quite seriously, that man would never land on the moon because the moon was covered by a thick vegetation. Any craft that landed on the moon, said my correspondent, would bounce off the spongy layer of vegetation and fall into the sun, or else it would disappear into the impenetrable lunar jungle! Nothing Carlos Allende ever said was any wilder than that.

The U.S. Navy has denied that they ever conducted the Philadelphia Experiment, or having any interest in the Allende letters, or Morris K. Jessup. Despite repeated inquiries naval authorities have treated the whole affair as a silly business.

Could the Navy and/or other official bodies be "covering up"? Is it all part of a "conspiracy of silence"? Many have claimed that this is exactly what has happened. These days it seems that government conspiracies and cover-ups are practically routine. But when they do occur there are usually leaks and rumors from several sources. Here, the only information we have on the subject comes from a single source—the letters sent to Jessup—and that is hardly the sort of source to inspire much confidence.

160

Charles Berlitz added to the original Allende story by saying that the destroyer was subjected to a degaussing equipment, and that that is what made it vanish. Degaussing, in fact, does make ships or other things disappear, but only magnetically; wrapping a ship with electrically charged cables neutralizes its magnetism. The purpose is to enable a ship to pass over magnetically operated mines without setting them off. But to imply that degaussing a ship would make it disappear from sight, and perhaps even reappear hundreds of miles away, is simply nonsense. It is possible, however, that the whole incredible legend of the Philadelphia Experiment may have started in just such a confusion. But there is no reason for the confusion to persist any longer; the U.S. Navy did not accidentally discover a force which makes things disappear mysteriously.

One often hears the theory that people, or ships, or planes which disappear mysteriously have fallen victim to a "space-time warp," or "anomaly"—that they have disappeared into "another dimension."

One occasionally reads "explanations" like this one offered by James Raymond Wolfe, who lectures on strange phenomena:

"With a particle almost infinitely small, but having an almost infinite mass, the volume of space distorted would be small, and so would the dimension of time. But we do not need a great time distortion, just enough to nudge the target hit a little further ahead of us on the time track. Or maybe a little behind us.

"If such particles occasionally drill into us from outer space, probability tells us that one or some of them will inevitably hit a plane or a ship or a person, knocking it out of its time orbit."

But this easy talk of time warps and other dimensions or getting knocked out of the "time orbit" is really the stuff of science-fiction. Of course, it is *possible* that various things are swallowed up in a space-time warp, just as it is possible that people are being kidnapped by extraterrestrials—or, as someone else suggested, spirited away by representatives of a super-civilization that lives undetected, and unsuspected, beneath the ocean.

Less than two hundred years ago in parts of Ireland, England, and France, if a person disappeared mysteriously it was assumed that he or she had been "taken" by the fairy folk. Being "taken" meant that the person had been carried off bodily by the fairies and made to dwell forever in the underground realm of the fairies. So it is *possible* that Judge Crater and the crew of the *Mary Celeste* and many of the others that we have discussed in this book have, in fact, been kidnapped by the fairies. The fairies, according to legend, could render themselves invisible when they wanted. But the idea sounds pretty silly, because we no longer believe in fairies (at least most of us don't). Yet there is not a shred more evidence for the existence of space-time warps or extraterrestrial kidnappers than there is for the existence of fairy land and the fairy folk. They just sound more up to date and scientific.

We all love mysteries, and the bigger the mystery the more we love it. Therefore, the idea that all of these mysterious disappearances are due to some strange and bizarre, utterly unworldly, underlying cause is tremendously attractive and satisfying. But it isn't necessarily true. Often mysteries have been "manufactured" by leaving out certain important facts, or, as in the case of the Philadelphia Experiment, they may be complete fabrications.

I'm not trying to imply that there are no mysterious disappearances. Of course there are—hundreds of them, thousands

162

probably. In this book we have taken only samples from the vast pool of strange and eerie tales of people and things that disappeared. Many of these cases will never be solved. The most likely reason is that the relevant information has been lost, but we cannot entirely rule out the possibility that the explanation is really unworldly and beyond our comprehension. Still, we ought to have the humility and good sense to admit that in many cases we simply don't know what happened or why, and we should stop there. There is no need to go chasing after the wildest and woolliest explanation around, just because it is exciting, and because it promises to tie up all the loose ends in one neat, though unprovable, package.

The desire to try and tie it all together is enormous. Charles Fort was consumed by such a desire, even though he often tried to act as if he really had no grand theories at all, but merely collected odd and unexplainable events. The proof of his passion to tie it all together, is undeniable. After listing a large number of odd events, including disappearances, he wrote:

"But the underlying oneness in all confusions."

Several other times he referred to *"Underlying oneness"* and he always put the words in italics to emphasize them. What this *oneness* was Fort never said. Probably he never knew. It was just the feeling that was important. Latter day devotees of mysterious disappearances—many of whom call themselves Forteans in honor of Charles Fort—have the same feeling.

The ancient Greeks had a tale about a quite nasty fellow named Procrustes. He was said to own two beds, one short and one long. He would capture people and force them to lie down in one of the two beds. If they were too short for the bed, he would try to stretch them out. If they were too long, he would lop off whatever portions hung over.

A lot of Forteans are guilty of Procrustian tendencies—not with people, of course, for they are not murderers—but with facts and theories. They have been known to stretch some facts in order to fit a theory, and discard others that pointed to alternative explanations, in their search for the *"Underlying oneness"* they feel must be behind it all.

Let us have our mysteries by all means. Let us ponder them, speculate on them, argue over them—in short, let us enjoy them. But just because they remain mysteries does not mean that we have to turn the world upside down in order to try and explain them.

Selected Bibliography

Berlitz, Charles. *The Bermuda Triangle*. New York: Doubleday, 1974.

Bowman, John S. *The Quest for Atlantis*. New York: Doubleday, 1971.

Churchill, Allen. *They Never Came Back*. New York: Doubleday, 1960.

Cohen, Daniel. *Mysterious Places*. New York: Dodd, Mead, 1969.

————. *Voodoo, Devils, and the New Invisible World*. New York: Dodd, Mead, 1972.

De Camp, L. Sprague. *Lost Continents*. New York: Gnome Press, 1954.

Dempewolff, Richard F., ed. *Lost Cities and Forgotten Tribes*. New York: Hearst Books, 1974.

Donnelly, Ignatius. *Atlantis—The Antediluvian World*, rev. New York: Harper, 1949.

Ebon, Martin, ed. *The Riddle of the Bermuda Triangle*. New York: New American Library, 1975.

Flammonde, Paris. *The Age of Flying Saucers*. New York: Hawthorn, 1971.

Fort, Charles. *The Books of Charles Fort*. New York: Holt, 1941.

Gaddis, Vincent. *Invisible Horizons*. Philadelphia: Chilton, 1963.

Goodwin, John. *This Baffling World*. New York: Hart Publishing, 1968.

Gould, Rupert. *Enigmas*. New Hyde Park, N.Y.: University Books, 1965.

SELECTED BIBLIOGRAPHY

Hapgood, Charles H. *Maps of the Ancient Sea Kings.* Philadelphia: Chilton, 1966.

Keel, John A. *Our Haunted Planet.* New York: Fawcett, 1971.

Kusche, Lawrence David. *The Bermuda Triangle Mystery—Solved.* New York: Harper, 1975.

O'Donnell, Elliott. *Strange Disappearances.* New Hyde Park, N.Y.: University Books, 1972.

Ronan, Colin. *Lost Discoveries.* New York: McGraw-Hill, 1973.

Sanderson, Ivan T. *Invisible Residents.* New York: World, 1970.

Shapiro, Harry L. *Peking Man.* New York: Simon & Schuster, 1974.

Spencer, John Wallace. *Limbo of the Lost.* Westfield, Mass.: Phillips Publishing Co., 1970.

Tompkins, Peter. *Secrets of the Great Pyramid.* New York: Harper & Row, 1971.

Winer, Richard. *The Devil's Triangle.* New York: Bantam, 1974.

Index

167

169

The Author

DANIEL COHEN is a free-lance writer and former managing editor of *Science Digest* magazine. He has written numerous books for adults and young readers on subjects ranging from science to the supernatural. His previous books include *In Search of Ghosts*, *The Magic Art of Foreseeing the Future*, and *The Mysteries of Reincarnation*. He also appears frequently on radio and television and has lectured at colleges and universities throughout the country.

Mr. Cohen is a native of Chicago and holds a degree in journalism from the University of Illinois. He lives with his wife, who is also a writer, their daughter, and a collection of cats and dogs in Port Jervis, New York.